_1984_

writing

THE PERSONAL VOICE

WRITING

THE PERSONAL VOICE

Jill Wilson Cohn

California State College, Bakersfield

HARCOURT BRACE JOVANOVICH, INC.

New York   Chicago   San Francisco   Atlanta

ISBN: 0-15-597787-3

Library of Congress Catalog Card Number: 74-33749

Printed in the United States of America

preface

This book is based on several premises about writing, language, and learning that will be explored in more detail in the chapters that follow. I shall summarize these assumptions here. First, I believe that the process of learning to write is similar to the process of maturation, during which we develop more complex relationships with the world around us. Thus, the theory of this book is implicit in the sequence of writing experiences. In the early chapters students are asked to explore the details of their immediate experiences with themselves and their world, to discover appropriate language, and to develop authentic voices. Next they examine their interactions with place and their relationships with people. In the later chapters they are asked to consider issues and ideas and to examine the sources of their opinions. This organization points up the parallel between our growth as individuals and our development as writers. As we grow outward from our immediate experience with self, we perceive, consider, and respond to the increasing diversity of the world around us.

A second premise of the book is that learning to write is an ongoing process that continues throughout our lives. There is therefore no "magic" formula that will guarantee an effective paper. The writing process involves the interrelationship of three major elements: a writer, a topic, and an audience. Language, a fourth element, is so integral a part of the writing process that we sometimes have difficulty considering it in isolation, for language is the medium through which we relate to the things, places, and people in our world. This book asks students to consider the nature of language and the way we use it to shape our lives. In addition, students who use this book should learn to participate fully as an audience for other student writers. Learning to be responsive, intelligent, sensitive readers will help students to become more perceptive and skillful writers.

I have written this book for both instructors and students. There is no separate instructor's manual because none of my advice is intended exclusively for instructors. I believe writing classes function best when we all work together as writers and as audiences to explore, experiment, respond, and offer advice. Likewise, no section of the book deals exclusively with grammar, usage, or writing conventions. Instructors or students who need such a resource may consult a supplementary handbook.

I would encourage classes to regard this book not as a programed text but as a guide and a source of motivation. Some readers may disagree with my discussion of a paper and choose to write a rebuttal. Others may decide to create their own assignments rather than follow my suggestions. As students respond to this book, share their own writing, and offer helpful suggestions to others, they will be contributing to a creative group effort. In a sense, then, every writing class creates its own book.

Although my name appears as author of this book, credit and thanks should be extended to all my students at Michigan State University, Western Michigan University, and California State College, Bakersfield—those whose papers are reprinted in this book and those whose papers are still in my files. Without them I never could have written it. Nearly all the work reprinted here was written by students —freshmen, juniors, graduate students. Not all the papers are polished; none are flawless. All of them, however, are at least partially, if not fully, infused with authentic voices of students talking about feelings, places, people, or ideas that are meaningful to them.

My appreciation also extends to Edward P. J. Corbett and John F. Butler for reviewing an early draft of the manuscript; to Alan B. Hollingsworth for first providing me with an opportunity to explore and develop new approaches to the teaching of writing; to Jean Malmstrom and Steve Judy for their encouragement when it was greatly needed; to Robert Wise for his willingness to read and discuss theories of writing; and especially to Barbara Hamilton for her continued advice, her intellect, and her perceptive wit. I thank my husband Kim for his encouragement and his patience when I typed at midnight, and my daughter Carinda, who was so intrigued with my endeavors that she began to write several books of her own.

Finally, my appreciation extends to Gordon Fairburn for his counsel and support; to Albert Richards and Christina Norum for their thoughtful editing; and to Carole Harden, Penny Vorhees, and Vivian Cochneuer for their careful typing.

JILL WILSON COHN

contents

ix

writing as experience

"I want to learn how to write a good paper in good English." The comment came from a young woman sitting in the far left section of the circle of students in my introductory composition class. It was the first day of the term. The September sun that flooded the room bolstered my beginning-of-the-year enthusiasm.

"What do you mean by 'good' English and what is a 'good' paper?" I asked in return. Feet shuffled. Desks were adjusted. I glanced around the circle, silently guessing why each had come to college and whether any of them had ever enjoyed writing. They were all either freshmen or sophomores. According to the index cards I had just collected, only four of them were English majors. I wondered how writing had been taught in their high schools and elementary schools. Most of them probably had been writing in classes for nearly twelve years of their lives. I was keenly interested in their ideas about writing, but I saw from their faces that they had interpreted my question as a rhetorical one.

"A good paper," the young woman replied in an offhand manner. "You know, one that is properly written in complete sentences with correct spelling."

I looked around the room again. "Do you all agree with that definition?" I asked the class. Most of the faces were still impassive. A few students stared out the window. One or two looked puzzled, probably wondering what the point of the discussion was. With a little urging on my part, the class added other criteria for a good paper. Collectively, they decided that a good paper was written in complete sentences and paragraphs, with correct spelling; had an introductory and a concluding statement; was well organized, clearly supported, and properly punctuated.

No one mentioned the topic of the paper. No one mentioned the audience. No one mentioned that writers should have something they want to say. No one discussed the purpose of the paper. And no one indicated that the form of a paper might grow from the function of the paper. The responses offered in this class differed in no way from the criteria suggested that same week by the seniors in my English methods class. Evidently, four years of college had not changed anyone's views about writing.

I have shared this story with you because I want you to begin thinking about what good writing is. This book is written to help you explore some ideas about the process of writing, about yourselves, and about the uses of language. I hope you will discover, through your own writing and the writing of others, that composition is not merely a fixed pattern of words arranged on a page according to specific rules. Writing is not merely properly punctuated sentences or correctly organized paragraphs. Writing is, as James Moffett has said, "somebody talking to someone about something." This definition may sound simplistic to you, but it extends the process of writing beyond the merely mechanical. When we conceive of writing as somebody saying something to someone, we begin to consider ourselves as writers, we consider the person or persons in our audience, and we consider the topic or content of our message. *How* we write the message, that is, what we choose to include, what we choose to omit, what language we use, what format we select, and what tone we establish, depends on the tripartite structure of author, topic, and audience.

Below are excerpts from three papers, all written by the same student for different audiences. Notice that the language, form, and tone of each excerpt are dependent on the writer's relation to her topic and her audience. The first selection is a private journal entry in which the student, using free association, writes about her early childhood.

Childhood. Rolling tar balls at five or riding my own horse. It was a status symbol—like being able to play the piano in the seventh grade. My brother, a year older and always around with the neighborhood gang. I trailed along. Dick and I played with matches twice. Once in a wheat field and again out in the pasture. Almost got caught that time. Smoked curled up against the sky. We ran back and carried water from the creek in old rusty cans. Falling in the creek in the spring. Bloodsuckers, poison ivy and the stink pond. I don't remember lavished affection. No hugs, kisses, etc. Dad is the strongest person in the world. Mom is always there and can be pleaded with. Never Dad. My protest movement. I put burrs in her nylons once. Up on the roof I hid a typewriter tablet and used to go up there and draw to be alone. . . .

This selection is a random collection of fragmented memories. The writer is close both to her topic and to her audience. She has first-hand knowledge of her topic (her childhood), and she has a limited, private audience (herself). Her purpose is to revive and record her memories. The usual conventions regarding sentence structure and punctuation are not rigidly enforced, nor are they necessary. The tone is intimate and relaxed—even rambling. The context in which this paper was written does not require the author to substantiate her opinion or to follow any conventional format.

The audience for the next excerpt is not the writer herself but a classmate. This time the writer offers critical response and specific suggestions for improving the other student's paper.

I was disappointed in your last two paragraphs. They seem to me to be just an unnecessary addition and really anti-climactic. You don't prepare us for this departure into fantasy anywhere in the paper. The picture of the bears and the dump, while nicely drawn, has no hint of this magical, almost whimsical mood. Further, the episode with the fast car and your incredulous, half-humorous reaction to the driver's message provide a quick and refreshing turn in the story. I don't think the reader can sustain a second twist in the story. It only detracts from the moment of climax, which can effectively end the story.

It is clear that the structure and language of the second example differ from the first, which is natural, since the author's relationship to both topic and audience has changed. The writer is personal and direct, but she uses conventional sentence structure and takes care to refer to specific details in the paper she is criticizing. Her comments are not intended as formal or public criticism, however. She writes in the first person and speaks directly to the author of the other paper. It is clear that the message is intended primarily, perhaps exclusively, for her classmate. It is also clear that the comments are offered as opinions, not as facts nor as public pronouncements. Note, too, that since both the writer and her audience are familiar with the paper under discussion, there is no need to quote lengthy passages from it.

The last excerpt is from a short story intended for a wider audience. Though the writer may have known someone like Jennifer, the main character of the story, the central intention here is not to relate directly the personal opinion or experience of the writer. The passage is written not in the first person but in the third person; the personality and presence of the author are much more removed.

Jennifer gratefully sipped her iced tea. The afternoon was hot and dry, and she felt its weight like an unseen hand bearing down on her mind. Placing her glass on the arm of her patio chair, she looked up, and in a sweeping glance took in the view before her. Her brows knit as she realized how brown and ragged the lawn had become. The carefully laid sod covering the gentle sloping lawn that fell from the flagstone patio, even the hedge that marked the boundaries of their property, needed attention. Turning in her chair, she was surprised by the disorder that had begun to curl around the edges of the terraced garden that flanked the right side of the patio. She sat up in her chair a little, took in the landscape deliberately for another second, and made a mental note to hire a gardener the first of next week.

> She didn't feel up to gardening now and wasn't sure, anyway, just how to approach these ragged blooms. Jason had never allowed anyone but himself to care for the yard.

This selection is filled with concrete details. Jennifer and her surroundings are vividly depicted. The writing context here necessitates the detail, since the audience for this paper is diverse and distant from the writer. She cannot assume that her audience will picture Jennifer as she wants them to, so she must create the scene. She must choose details that evoke the desired response from her readers. As the story unfolds, the writer must also provide, either directly or indirectly, any information necessary to understand the story. In other words, the writing context for this paper differs from that of the previous excerpts. In each of the selections the language, form, tone, and even the sentence structure depend on the author's relationship to her topic and to her audience.

Perhaps you have already noticed that it is difficult to speak about writing without also discussing language, for it is language that links writer, topic, and audience. You might want to think of language as a fourth element of the writing process. Language is, after all, the medium through which we communicate and through which we relate to the world. The importance of language is clear when we consider how our lives are immersed in words. Have you ever imagined what your life would be like without written and spoken language? Think for a moment how you would experience a week, a day, or even an hour without language. You would not understand spoken sounds. You could not chat with friends or use the telephone. You would not be able to understand song lyrics or your favorite television drama. Nor would you be able to read anything—books, newspapers, letters, or posters. You could not read the titles on a theater marquee or the captions for cartoons. You would not be able to name the things you see around you. In fact, you would not even know your own name. But that is not all. Language is not restricted simply to what we say and write. Each of us also has an inner stream of language constantly flowing in his or her head. We "talk to ourselves." This inner language is usually disconnected. It is a never-ceasing flow of words often tumbling forth in random fashion. The words continue even when we sleep. It is next to impossible to shut off this inner language. Try it sometime.

Language is so important to our lives that we could view words as the very texture of our experience. Edward Sapir, the famous linguist, suggested that language "interpenetrates" with experience. James Miller explores this concept in more detail.

> Words do not simply accompany experience; more frequently they *are* the experience, or are its primary content. We live surrounded by language, inside and outside us. It can strangle and suffocate us, or it can connect and link, strengthen and renew us. Language, then, is far more than mere communication; it is indeed a kind of creation. With it we make our world and ourselves. Through our daily linguistic encounter with the world, we proclaim our identities, shape our lives, and (in some small or big way) leave our impress on the world.[1]

Consider for a moment how language shapes our lives. We are all keenly aware of ourselves—our bodies, our emotions, our thoughts, our desires. But only language enables us to communicate this awareness both to ourselves and to others. "I think, therefore I am," said Descartes. Implicit in that statement is the importance of language: I think (and I communicate thoughts to myself), therefore I am.

We not only communicate our self-awareness with language, but that awareness is in part shaped by our language. Language enables us to label our emotions and thoughts—to discriminate one feeling from another and one idea from another. We are all familiar with the statement, "I know what I mean, but I don't know how to say it." Finding suitable language to state our meaning helps us to clarify and formalize our thoughts. In this sense language helps us to discover and create our selves.

Language also enables us to establish our relationship to places and to other people. The language we use to describe a place helps define the meaning of that place in our lives. A par-

---

[1] *Word, Self, Reality: The Rhetoric of Imagination* (New York: Dodd, Mead & Co., 1972), p. 15.

ticular building may be a house to one person but a home to another. You may own a rustic cabin that your neighbors think is a dilapidated shack. Think of all the words that might designate the place where a person lives: *home, pad, castle, digs, residence, dump, domicile, nest,* are only a few. The word chosen specifies a relationship between the person and the place.

Language also helps us to create and sustain our relationship with other people. Words allow us to discern our feelings toward others. We love, hate, suspect, respect, fear, trust, ostracize, and mock people. The words not only serve as a medium of communication but also help us identify, shape, and give meaning to those relationships.

This interpenetration of language and experience perhaps explains why language is so personal. Since we each experience life individually, it is not surprising that our use of language is distinctive. Each of us has a personal voice, which is characterized, for example, by the words, tone, syntax, and inflections we use. The way we speak and write strongly influences the image we project to others. Our voices are part of us. This is clearly illustrated by comedians who impersonate famous people: a few physical gestures and facial expressions are usually part of the act, but the key to a successful imitation is the characterization of the obvious features of the person's voice and speech patterns.

Each of you has a personal speaking voice. You can probably identify many of your friends by their voices. Similar personal qualities can also be extended (if they are not already there) to your written voice. This is not to say that your written voice needs to imitate your speaking voice. The spoken language and the written language do differ, and they are governed by different conventions. When you speak, you do not have to spell; when you write, you do not have to concern yourself with intonations. Speaking is a more natural act for most of us than writing is. Writing requires a conscious and controlled effort. Despite these differences, I would encourage you to regard writing as a natural extension of yourself.

Making writing a natural act, however, should not lead to carelessness. The process of putting words on paper requires concentration and effort. As you write you will almost certainly have to change your wording or omit part of what you have written.

This revision, paradoxically, is both a frustrating and a satisfying aspect of writing. You may have to cross out or rephrase sections of a paper; and you may have to struggle to find the words you want; but when you finish, you have a permanent record. If you like what you have written, you will be pleased, for it will be an extension and expression of yourself.

If you begin to think of language or writing as an extension of yourself—as a medium through which you relate to the world and give meaning to your experience—you will be more fully aware of the centrality and importance of language in your life. Language is powerful and influential. Words can and do change our lives. With words we express ourselves; we relate to others; we create imaginary lives; we share past experiences; we react to the present; and we reach out to the future.

You may already be aware of the power of the spoken word. The written word, however, has both power and permanence. I don't think I fully appreciated how my own writing might shape and record my reality until my freshman year in college. The experience is still etched in my memory, and I think it is worth sharing with you in detail. My first week at the University of Michigan was filled with orientation activities. A group of about twenty of us, awed and nervously excited, trailed after our sophomore guide through a seemingly endless labyrinth of buildings, hallways, and sidewalks. Later in the afternoon, we were ushered into a stark classroom filled with arm desks. We sweated and fidgeted our way through a battery of tests. That evening the entire entering freshman class gathered in the auditorium to be officially greeted by the appropriate administrative officials. I don't remember who was the featured speaker—the president or the vice president, I suppose; I don't even remember what he looked like. What I do remember are the sensations I felt and the thoughts I had as I sat in the audience. Though uncertain of my own capabilities, I nevertheless felt as though I were poised on a threshold of endless magnificent opportunities. Anything was possible, now that I was in college. I might fail, but I might succeed. The world might be mine. This initial sense of anticipation reverberated throughout the evening's formalities. Most of what was said that evening has retreated into oblivion. However, what struck me then and still remains vivid in my memory was a brief comment made by one of the speakers, who was discussing the value and challenge of getting an education. When he mentioned the act of writing, he said that one of the loneliest and most challenging moments in our lives is when we sit alone with a pen in hand and a blank sheet of paper in front of us. That moment, he added, also held the opportunity for creativity, fulfillment, even power. The image struck me then because the comment reinforced my own personal state of mind that evening. Perhaps I saw my life as a blank sheet of paper—trite though the metaphor was. The potential for shaping—indeed creating—my future by enrolling in courses, by selecting my friends, by reading books, by joining organizations, by preparing for a profession, was not unlike the creative act of putting words on paper.

This is not to say that writing about something—about life—is the same as living it. We cannot literally create our futures on paper. Writing isn't a substitute for life. But that evening I understood how writing could contribute to the discovering, shaping, and recording of life. Writing enables us to capture and structure our experience: what we imagine, what we hope for in the future, what we think about in the present, what we remember from the past are embedded in language and can be clarified and recorded if we write them down. Life itself—your first camp experience, the day your dog died, Christmas holidays at grandma's, your bout with the measles, your senior prom—is composed of fleeting moments that endure only in your shifting, often fading, memories. Even our opinions and thoughts fluctuate in our memories. In writing, however, we can give a shape to our experience; we can permanently record our thoughts, our dreams, our lives.

That evening in the auditorium I began to regard the written word with new respect. Even now when I am faced with the task of committing words to paper (as I was when I began this book), I think of the potential of the situation: a writer, a pen, and a sheet of blank paper. You might be amused to learn that the words in this chapter did not come forth smoothly in uninterrupted precision. In fact, I thought it might be valuable to share with you my experiences while trying to begin this chapter. Published textbooks on composition are usually polished and professional. By example, they seem to suggest that writing is easily, quite naturally achieved. "Look," the author seems to say, "I have done it and other students have done it. Just follow the rules and you too can do it." Yet the act of composing is seldom so simple. Perhaps it will be comforting to know that even an author of a composition text does not simply sit down and whip out a polished manuscript.

This chapter, for example, got off to several false starts. I began to think about it during spring quarter, assured that, once the year was over and I had some free time, I could finish it easily. After submitting my final grades and clearing my desk, I took a well-earned weekend break. When Monday morning came, there I was—at my desk in a quiet office, staring at a blank sheet of paper. I found that I had nothing to say! For the past few weeks I had been occupied with other matters—student evaluations, literature projects, graduate theses. I hadn't been giving careful thought to what I wanted to say about composition. That Monday I spent the morning in a series of displacement activities. I would write a paragraph, stare out the window, get a cup of coffee, chat with my friend next door, and answer phone calls. Then I would try another paragraph or jot down assorted points I wished to make. A few months earlier the chapter would have been easy to write. I was involved then with thinking, discussing, reading, and teaching composition. Now I found myself in a fallow period, and the longer I took to get started, the more uneasy I felt. Finally, I began reading some student papers; then I spent a few days reading essays and excerpts from books about language, imagination, and the process of composing. I began, in short, to stimulate my mind. I talked with my colleague next door about the uses and misuses of language. I dictated some isolated thoughts. Before long my ideas were alive and moving once again. I found that I had recovered not only the content of what I wanted to say but also the interest and desire to communicate that content to you. Even at this stage the words didn't fall neatly in place, however. Sentences were crossed out; alternate wordings were inserted. And sometimes when I couldn't think of the right word, I would leave blank spaces. When I was interrupted by phone calls or visitors to my office, I would often lose the direction of my thoughts. The words would escape, and I would have to struggle to regain the appropriate language. This procedure has prevailed throughout the writing of this book. When I finished a section, I would let it sit for a few days and then reread it. Sometimes I revised a section several times; other times I knew a section should be revised, but I just didn't feel like doing it. I would avoid the task for a while, then finally I would rework it. What helped me through these rough places, ultimately, was my desire to communicate with you. Without that desire and commitment, I would have neither started nor finished this book.

I'm telling you all this because I want to emphasize that writing is an ongoing process that we continue to improve throughout our lives. Writers are continually learning to write and continually revising their work. Consequently, there is no formula that, once learned by a student, will guarantee that he or she will write with clarity, precision, or force. Despite this fact, composition texts and rhetoric classes sometimes lead students to believe that such a formula exists. Perhaps the greatest disservice a writing course can do is to lead students to believe that good writing results if one learns the rules or the fundamentals. Many dead and dull papers have been produced by following the rules. Writing conventions are important, but a knowledge of them does not assure good writing. Nor does knowledge of certain forms or modes of writing, or knowledge of certain techniques of writing, assure good writing. Many composition texts are organized according to such forms or techniques. Students using these books practice writing paragraphs or structuring sentences. They practice using metaphors, personification, or allusion. When they write complete papers, they use professional models of the personal essay, the critical essay, the persuasive essay, or the research paper as a guide. Perhaps you have already taken a course in which you used such books.

This book has a different organization and a different premise about the writing process. It begins by asking you to explore yourself and your world, to experiment with the rich potential of your language, and to be aware of the responses of your audience. You will be encouraged to communicate sensations, experiences, and ideas that interest you. The organization of the book attempts to parallel your personal growth. The early chapters ask you to consider your emotions, your experiences with self and with place. Later you are encouraged to write about your relationship with people, both individually and in groups. Finally, you are encouraged to write about ideas and issues that may be even further removed from your immediate personal experience. Fiction writing is also included because it represents an interesting combination of subjective experience and external form. Since fiction writers often objectify personal experience, the fictional mode offers an appropriate culmination of the other writing experiences you will have.

As you move from writing about the self to writing about places, people, and ideas, you will want to be concerned with the form and the mechanics of your writing. But repeatedly I will be encouraging you to consider these elements within the total writing context of someone talking to somebody about something.

You will notice that most of the writing selections reproduced in this book were not written by professionals, but are student papers written for a composition class. Except for spelling and occasional minor additions or deletions, these papers have not been professionally edited (much to the initial dismay of my editors). You probably will be able to find strengths and weaknesses in each of the selections. They are offered not as models but as sources for discussion and perhaps as motivation for your own writing.

You will also notice that the student writers vary greatly in age and experience. Increasingly, writing classes are attracting a wide spectrum of students. I have had grandmothers, Vietnam veterans, young mothers, and recently divorced men in my introductory composition classes, and I've had young, unsophisticated twenty-one-year-olds in my graduate classes. The papers therefore range widely in topic and focus.

No magic formula for success in writing is offered here. I don't believe such a formula exists. But perhaps this book will help you revitalize or reawaken your sensitivity to the richness of language and to the possibilities of extending yourself in writing. If you write often, if you care about your writing, if you read your work and the work of others, if you talk to others about your writing and revise it accordingly, your writing will improve. Most important, however, is that through your writing you may discover, clarify, and record your emotions, experiences, and ideas. You may, in fact, use language to give design and meaning to your life.

response to writing

If, as I believe, writing is learned in the same basic way other activities are learned—by doing and by heeding what happens—then it is possible to describe ideal teaching practices in this way and compare them with some current practices. Ideally a student would write because he was intent on saying something for real reasons of his own and because he wanted to get certain effects on a definite audience. He would write only authentic kinds of discourse such as exist outside of school. A maximum amount of feedback would be provided him in the form of audience response. That is, his writing would be read and discussed by this audience, who would also be the coaches. This response would be candid and specific. Adjustments in language, form, and content would come as the writer's response to his audience's response. This instruction would always be individual, relevant and timely. These are precisely the virtues of feedback learning that account for its great success.

JAMES MOFFETT
Teaching the Universe of Discourse

Each of you as a student in a writing class has a dual role: you are both writer and audience. In both roles you must actively engage yourself with others. As writer you extend yourself; as audience you attend and respond. Emphasis on these dual roles and on the interaction between writers and audience is both desirable and productive because a beginning writer is often only partly aware of an audience. You may assume, for example, that your audience thinks and feels as you do and has had experience similar to your own. As a result you may omit important information, neglect to include specific details, or fail to provide sufficient support for your views. Often you will not know whether you have assumed too much or said enough until you hear your audience responding.

Responding as a reader also benefits you as a writer. When you become actively involved in responding and offering advice to others, you may learn a good deal about your own writing and the writing process. You may also become more aware of the expectations you have as a reader. You may notice and comment on ambiguous statements, lack of coherence, misleading punctuation, inappropriate language, or poor organization. As you become more aware of what you expect as a reader, you may also learn how to sharpen your skills as a writer.

Learning to respond intelligently and constructively to writing is no easy task, however. In fact, your responsibility as an audience, though different, is as difficult and demanding in its own way as your task as a writer. You have to consider what it is you wish to say and how you wish to say it; you must also decide what criteria or standards you wish to apply to the writing. As you learn to experience, to respond to, and to evaluate another's writing, you will be developing your personal standards of good or effective writing.

It is neither sufficient nor desirable that you simply adopt an instructor's or another student's opinion of what is good, effective, or successful writing. You will want instead to discover your own views about writing and in doing so you probably will discover that good writing *depends* on many factors.

As a reader, you are challenged to be positive and supportive and at the same time to be specific, helpful, and accurate. Responsible criticism requires attention, care, and consideration; it also requires information and opinions. You will want to read papers attentively, consider your responses thoughtfully, and write your informed opinions carefully. The task is indeed a difficult one, requiring a good deal of practice. Not long ago in my graduate writing class I asked each student to write a critical response to another student's paper. One of the students—who wrote competently—came into my office the next day looking concerned and anxious. He had been trying unsuccessfully to compose a helpful response. He thought the paper was poorly written, but he could not bring himself to express his honest opinion; nor did he know how to modify that opinion. This was the first time in five years of college that any instructor had asked him to respond critically to another student's work, and he was completely at a loss.

You too may be uncertain about how to comment on another student's work. First, you should remember that the skill of responding to writing, like any other skill, improves with practice. There are several ways to begin. You might agree as a class, for example, to give only positive comments on the first few papers; you can say what you like about the paper and why. Positive responses will encourage a writer. Or you might begin by mentioning one or two strengths and one or two weaknesses of a given paper. This alternative will encourage writers but will also suggest ways to improve their writing. It is usually helpful at this beginning stage to respond by opening broad areas of possible discussion, such as the writer's intent, the central concern of the paper, or the choice of topic. To prepare for class discussion you might ask yourself a series of questions after reading a paper. Is the experience familiar? Has anything similar happened to you? Is the topic too familiar or the style too informal? Are more details needed? Do you understand what the writer is saying? Do you understand the emotions or the opinions? Do you agree with them? If you do not agree, what do you think could be changed, omitted, or added that would be more convincing for you? Are there sentences or examples that are confusing or misleading? What questions do you have after reading the paper? How does this paper differ from the other papers you have read on the same topic? The first attempts to answer these introductory questions may be clumsy and perhaps even superficial. What is important is to keep trying to refine, particularize, and support your responses. It is not easy.

The initial responses to papers in my introductory writing classes are often general and supportive; sometimes they are defensive. Beginning writers, especially, feel uncomfortable or even presumptuous when they criticize the work of their peers. The criticized writers also feel self-conscious. The atmosphere established in the classroom greatly affects the outcome of these first hesitant offerings. At its best the environment in a writing class accommodates a variety of opinions, yet encourages honesty and requires tact. You can contribute to shaping such an atmosphere by offering constructive suggestions to the writer. As a writer, you can also help by soliciting responses to your own papers. Even a reticent audience is likely to respond to a direct question from the writer. Even if the papers are anonymous, you can ask the class specific questions without identifying yourself as the author. Hopefully, as you and your fellow writers gain confidence and experience, opinions will become more detailed and more clearly supported by specific references to the paper.

Once you become comfortable with initial responses, you can proceed toward a more detailed examination of a paper. You can begin by asking what the paper attempts to say. Does it fulfill the assignment? If not, what does it say or do? Are there sections that are confusing? If so, what could the author change, extend, or eliminate to clarify the paper? You can ask questions about the writer's choice of language. Is the language appropriate to the general tone and intent of the paper? Is the language too formal or too colloquial for the context? Are there words or phrases that seem out of place? Why do they seem out of place? Is there a first-person narrator in the paper? Is the view or opinion reliable? What could the writer do to sound more convincing? Are there any examples? Should there be? If there are, do they support the point? Is significant information overlooked by the writer? Should the paper include more detail? Does the paper have an organization that is appropriate to the general tone and intent of the paper?

The answers to these and other questions, of course, will vary from paper to paper, depending on the mode, tone, and intent. All these questions can best be discussed in the contexts of specific papers. The following examples of student writing differ distinctly in style and purpose. The comments about each may serve to illustrate some of the ways you can respond to writing.

The first paper was written as a character sketch for an introductory writing class. Students in other writing classes have been especially impressed by the concrete language and strong personal voice evident in the paper.

GRANDMA NELLIE

My Grandma Nellie sent me nutbread the other day. She sends almost as many packages as Mama does. Full of baked things and my younger cousin's A papers and pictures of mountains with poems to God on the back. I hide the pictures in my bottom drawer. At Thanksgiving she sent a box of fruit that was held up in the mail. I could smell it in the hall when it came and knew it was mine from her earlier letters. I have not written now for a long time, and her letter appears every week, reminding me of my neglect. During vacation she mentioned to Dad that she had seen me only once, and Dad made me take the car and drive all the way to Wadena to visit her. She's seventy and does not seem to be so old. But this Christmas she did not make as many kinds of candy as in other years.

There were dead leaves and acorns on her sidewalk in the fall when I was a kid. We were not allowed to play in the pile of Grandpa's cement gravel, but we could climb trees and run screaming in the dark yard if we were careful to show ourselves under the light at the window every few minutes. Little kids received the same punishment as older children; whining got them nowhere with Grandma. But I never saw her strike a child in my life; she pursed her lips and agreed only in principle when Mama spanked me for crossing the street.

Little Julie, the youngest grandchild, resembled a frog when she was five. Early in the morning she would run over from her house next door, and Grandma would waste many eggs before one pleased Julie. Grandpa would come in from morning walks and taunt Julie, for he said he liked to see her tonsils when she hollered. Grandma chided him for teasing such a little one, but Grandpa would smile his feeble smile and understand from the crinkling of Grandma's eyes, that Julie deserved it. Grandpa's eyes were red-rimmed, and when the wind blows dust, Grandma's eyes get blood-shot. Grandpa had once helped a bootlegger and Grandma had been a flapper. Her bosom has really grown some since. Now the younger grandchildren call her "the soft grandma." I know why, because she held me tightly and taught me "Humpty Dumpty" when Mama left me the first time.

There used to be a big family reunion at Grandma's house. Now they are held in the municipal park. Grandma would cook enough for an army; she had a knack for potato salad and beans baked with brown sugar. Once she was carrying a pan full of scalloped potatoes down the front steps and fell and broke her hip. All the relations helped get her to the hospital. I don't think she cried; I was playing at the fairgrounds and did not see. Her eyes were probably just watery, the way they get when she kisses me goodbye, and makes me feel so guilty. Her hip mended slowly; now she gets around as spryly as ever.

Grandma still combs and braids her light brown hair every morning. There is almost no gray in it. Grandpa sleeps all day in his rocker and took the battery out of the car so he wouldn't have to drive, but Grandma works as hard as ever, even though the school forgot to rehire her as head cook this year. She saw Halley's comet as a girl and expects to see it again. But this year there was not as much Christmas candy.

The richness of vivid detail is indeed impressive. Notice how effectively the writer uses contrasts of time, characters, and events to describe her grandmother. The details about the older grandmother are juxtaposed against information about the younger grandma, and at the same time the older narrator's point of view interprets the younger girl's experience. The opening paragraph introduces both the older grandma and the older narrator—that is, the eighteen-year-old writer introduces her seventy-year-old grandma and, indirectly, herself. Then she introduces the younger girl and younger woman in the second paragraph. It jumps back many years—perhaps twelve or fifteen—to recapture childhood memories associated with a younger grandma. In the third paragraph the writer continues to contrast information about the younger and older woman.

Contrasts between the behavior of the characters also help us understand Grandma. Mother spanks, but Grandma doesn't; Grandpa teases, but Grandma doesn't; Grandpa "sleeps all day in his rocker," but Grandma is still active and energetic.

The last paragraph is particularly effective and efficient in its use of language. We learn about Grandma's continuing vitality and optimism. She pays attention to her personal appearance— "Grandma still combs and braids her light brown hair every morning." She is energetic—"works as hard as ever." And she is looking forward to an even longer life—"She saw Halley's comet as a girl and expects to see it again." Yet the telltale signs are there—"the school forgot to rehire her as head cook." The implication here, of course, is that the school thinks Grandma is getting too old for the job. Most telling, however, is that "this year there was not as much Christmas candy." This final sentence, which echoes the last sentence of the opening paragraph, not only underscores grandma's declining health but effectively contributes to the unity of the paper.

Perhaps most effective and expressive in this portrayal of a warm and vital woman is the narrator's tone. She treats the grandmother with gentleness and respect (another tribute to the woman). Though she is evidently embarrassed by the "pictures of mountains with poems to God on the back," she does not destroy them or tell her grandmother to stop sending them. Instead she simply hides them "in my bottom drawer." Nor does the girl show resentment about having to visit the grandmother during vacation. Though she is guilty of neglect (a failure familiar to us all), she is neither callous nor insensitive. Her appreciation, concern, and love for Grandma Nellie are evident in the sharply focused memories. She cares enough to recreate the older woman's patience, strength, humor, and gentleness. She also cares enough to notice the subtle indications of her grandmother's failing health. (Now the reunions are held in the municipal park.)

Despite its obvious strengths, however, the paper does have some weaknesses that you may have noticed. At times the organization is confusing and misleading. Some readers find the transition between the first and second paragraphs abrupt. In addition, the second paragraph focuses on two apparently unrelated memories—playing and being punished. The third paragraph also opens abruptly; the first sentence is misleading because it apparently shifts emphasis from Grandma to Julie, and only when we reread do we understand why Julie is included. This paragraph also includes unrelated information: the grandparents' eyes, the past experiences as bootlegger and flapper respectively, and the softness of grandma's bosom are not clearly related. The intent apparently is to focus on their physical characteristics, but as readers we are not sure. I have commented on the strengths and weaknesses of this paper to illustrate the benefits of exploring both. Even a good paper can be of mixed quality. Discussing the weaknesses of a paper need not be embarrassing or humiliating for the writer but rather can be helpful and constructive.

The second paper was also written for an introductory writing class. The writer wanted to express her opinion on a topic of social importance.

ON THE MAKING OF CITIES

All day we saw them coming,
the trucks and truckers,
the caterpillars
    and cat-skinners.
The foremen and the workmen,
the asphalt spreaders
    in their dirty black trucks [1]

Farmington was a small town, a suburb held loosely by
Detroit, when we moved there fourteen years ago.
Actually, my family lived four miles from town in Kendallwood,
a newly formed subdivision whose unpaved, ungraveled

---

[1] All verse in this paper is from "The Day They Built the Road," words by Rod McKuen, copyright © 1967 by Warm Music. Additional text and editorial revision © 1972 by Rod McKuen. Published in the book, *And to Each Season*, by Simon & Schuster and Cheval Books. Reprinted by permission.

roads carved ribbons of mud into the rolling expanse of woods and fields. My brother and I flew kites in those fields on gusty days. And in the summer the grass grew so tall we could burrow through it to sneak a puff on our first cigarettes. Behind our house the trees grew tall and the undergrowth thick, forming a perfect place for climbing trees, building tree forts, and making paths. We learned to identify flowers, birds, animals, and trees because we were interested in the world around us.

After tramping through a quarter mile of forest, we would come upon a farm meadow with a brook filled with crayfish and catfish. We fished this spring-fed brook for hours on end, bringing home our treasured catch. For a while cows grazed in the meadow. Once, five cows broke through the fence, wandered through the woods, and trotted into our backyard to graze contentedly. My mother grabbed her broom and excitedly chased the cows back into the woods. They never came back.

Janet, one of my friends, lived on Twelve Mile Road, across from our subdivision. Together we galloped our imaginary horses across fields and over fences and formed an imaginary riding club. When we took a break from our "riding," we walked down a mile to Siler's Market for a bottle of pop or a candy bar. The old store carried every imaginable product, including a large assortment of candy. Jawbreakers were my favorite. Old Mr. Siler leaned casually over the counter, asking, "And what are we going to have today, my little ones?" Janet and I, our eyes large, silently held up our coke bottles. In a small voice I said, "Two cherry jawbreakers, too, please." Ringing up the sale, Mr. Siler gave each of us a red jawbreaker and with a smile told us to come again soon.

Another precious playground was Button's orchard. In the fall of the year, we climbed the apple tree, plucking juicy Delicious apples from them. Mr. Button didn't mind us playing there and eating his apples as long as we didn't destroy his beehives. Once in a while he gave us a ride on his tractor or wagon. We had to be careful, though, because poison ivy grew beneath the low-hanging branches of the trees.

> They'd cut straight through the north-
>   east field a month before.
> The steamshovel-harvest lay there still;
> Bent up cornstalks.
> Boulders with their shins skinned
> Now they'd come to finish up the job,
> To cut our lives up, too . . .

> It set me thinking about the dogs I'd chased
> Down by the yellow corn,
> The girls I'd walked home along the fence.
> Mostly the smell of the field,
> The sound of crows,
> The rattle of the field mice on the ground.

One day Janet told me she was going to move because an expressway was being built across their property. In a matter of months she had moved, and the house was destroyed. I awoke to the sound of machines every morning and fell asleep to them every night. Mom warned my brother and me of the danger of the workmen and the road equipment; we stayed away from the construction. Soon the fields and woods were flattened into an endless stretch of dirt. Dirt collected on our furniture; it seemed to come through the walls. Our lungs filled with smog made by the black diesel smoke and the oily wood smoke of burning wastes drenched in kerosene. Then the grinding of the caterpillars was replaced by the steady clanging and pounding of metal supports.

Soon the expressway was completed. Not only was the land where the expressway was built changed, but also the whole area. Land developers flocked to Farmington to develop subdivisions, shopping centers and apartments. Expensive subdivisions brought people out of the city to "country living." Schools became overcrowded and new ones were built. Shopping centers carried exclusive shops for suburban living. Apartments and townhouses popped up near the expressway exit to accommodate city workers who wanted to live in the suburbs. As we began to get closed in by a community of subdivisions, our house and our yard grew smaller and smaller. Our only consolation was the large tract of woods behind our house, and that, too, gave way to a subdivision.

Even Mr. Siler, who had bought his land in the 1940s for eight thousand dollars, sold it to Howard Johnson's for one-half million dollars. Mr. Button also sold out, and within a few months there will be an apartment community, complete with pool, golf course, and shopping center, where the orchards used to be. Within fifteen years the country had changed into the city; all because of a road.

Now we have moved twenty-five miles further from Detroit. Once again there are open fields and woods around us, a lake behind our house, and only the sounds of dogs and children are audible in the early morning. We are back where we were fifteen years ago. However, I heard there will be an expressway built nearby within the next four years. Then we will again watch the making of a city, the destruction of the country. How much farther must we move? How many more times *can* we move before the city closes in from all sides?

> Tomorrow we'd start smelling gasoline
>   and diesel smoke
> As the road came crashing through.
> Tomorrow . . .
> and tomorrow.
>
> Mama said it's just a road,
> But she knew, too
> That with the coming of the road
> Our lives would change
> It wouldn't be the same.
> And it wasn't.

As you consider this paper, you might think about the language, organization, examples, and details, plus the quality of the writer's voice. The essay develops inductively. The narrator begins by describing particular personal experiences and proceeds, through contrast, to develop her opinion about the effects of urban expansion. She neither makes vague generalizations nor does she quote impersonal facts. Rather than citing statistics about the number of displaced people or speaking directly about the way modern technology dehumanizes us, the writer simply describes her own experience and lets that speak for her.

Her central concern is not the construction of expressways, but what is lost in the process. To emphasize the loss, the narrator describes her childhood experiences in detail. She recreates in expressive, concrete language the place where she grew up—"unpaved, ungraveled roads carved ribbons of mud into the rolling expanse of woods and fields." She integrates specific activities such as flying kites and fishing with references to specific people—her brother, her friend Janet, and the storekeeper Mr. Siler. The personal involvement she has with people, events, and surroundings gives meaning to her hometown. All this is dramatically and irreversibly changed when the expressway invades. The integration of her world is interrupted and altered severely. Because she has been explicit in her description, we as readers can share her sense of loss and displacement.

The contrasting circumstances in the second half of the paper underscore this loss. There is no longer any individuality or intimacy. References to specific people or places are replaced by the noise of the machine, the gathering dust, and the ensuing hordes of people who pour into impersonal apartments and townhouses. Nearly everything is affected: Janet moves, Mr. Siler sells his store, the fields and trees are leveled, and finally the narrator's family moves.

The last paragraph unifies the essay by bringing us full circle back to a house in the country, but the circle is interrupted by the critical questions that end the essay. Only in the last paragraph does the writer directly refer to the central question posed by her essay: "How much farther must we move? How many more times *can* we move before the city closes in from all sides?"

Though the paper does indeed depict the loss and change caused by urban expansion, the writer never relies on abstract language. She does not generalize vaguely about the destructiveness of growing cities, the problems of overpopulation, or the necessity for space and privacy. Instead, the writing is specific and concrete. The organization and detail allow us to draw our own conclusions about urban expansion and its impact on the quality and privacy of American life.

You may have mixed reactions to the use of Rod McKuen's poem. Some readers do not like the poem; others feel that it too sharply interrupts the flow of the paper. They feel the poem should be either omitted or restricted to an introductory quotation. Yet the poem is relevant to the topic, and the writer has appropriately placed a section at the turning point of the essay. The poem is thus used both as a unifying device and as editorial commentary. By juxtaposing the poem and essay, additional meaning is given to both.

The next example, an autobiographical essay written for a freshman class, is more controversial than the previous two examples.

DILEMMA NO. 9

I don't believe they're asking to see my fur coat. God. This cannot be for real; I mean what *do* you say to your daughter when she returns from a half-day escapade with the Ann Arbor police?? Of course. You ask to see her new fur coat. Cripe. They really don't know where to begin. My own parents don't even know how to approach me. Ah me. The onset of the friendly parental confrontation scene. And I am to make the first move again. As usual. God. The setting is so pathetically familiar. Mother is giving me the back of her head under the ruse of peeling carrots and slamming dishes around. Sure Mom. You probably won't be speaking to me for a day or so anyhow. Dad, with a drink to stay his nerves, gazes through weary eyes from atop his lofty bar stool. I sprawl into a kitchen chair and proceed to scribble Nixon's face into oblivion from the cover of *Time* magazine. And try to feel guilty. Like about skipping school (because I only had two classes and the sun—oh wow—the sun!). Like about lousy grades (because I know I'm going into art and who gives a damn about Algebra II). Like about moral uncertainty (because can't you see that there are no such things as blanket morals and what's right for me may never be right for you??). I suppose I could wait for them to start the grilling but their beating around the bush is just a bit much. And this time, they are afraid. Really afraid. Conditioned to fear the cops and scared stiff of the drug scene, how could they be anything but up tight?? Would you believe communication barrier. Wow. This is going to be worse than I thought. I'll never be able to level with them. Never. Like I have to shelter my own parents from my actions. Shit. I guess they would have busted me for my thoughts sometime soon anyhow. You guys are really hung up on wanting me to groove on your middle-class values, huh. Yeah, yeah, yeah. I know. Give the Establishment a chance; drugs are "taboo" because they are illegal; guys with hair and bell bottoms are "weirdos"; premarital sex will ruin my "reputation"; get interested but not involved in what's happening around you; grades are of utmost importance always; college is for becoming a teacher and blah, blah, blah, blah. Spare me. Richard M. Nixon, I give you a pierced ear. Ah, Dad. You're about to ask me what really went on in Ann Arbor last night and this morning. God. As if that cop didn't have enough to say when he called you earlier today. To say that friend Jan got in a car accident as the result of a bad LSD trip; to say that I spent the night in a house that was at the center of a big Ann Arbor drug ring; to say that we weren't under arrest or in any serious trouble because he couldn't prove anything; to say that I was safe and had a ride home; but also to say that if I said I had no knowledge of the illicit "goings on," I was incredibly naive or simply B.S.-ing. Oh, God. If I have to even think about the whole scene much longer, I'm really going to crack. Telling it to the cops was raunchy enough. No, I do not drop acid and shoot heroin, Officer. No, I did not see the narcotics in the house. I kept falling asleep. Well, I came to Ann Arbor to buy a fur coat and see my roommate from school. No, we did not smoke marijuana. Then my friends are lying if they say we did? Sure, Officer. Bombard me with wild questions, fluster me, and then turn me against my friends. God. This is so totally absurd.

Detective Ackerman, you look like something out of a camping trip. Greasy hair in a 1950s pompadour. Dark plaid shirt, open with a graying undershirt. Mucky brown pants with one leg inside your boot and one out. And those beady little animal eyes. Yes sir. I am really impressed. You are fantastically rude, you know?? The truth is worth shit and I am getting really depressed. I so want to level with all of you —Mom, Dad, even you Detective Ackerman, you pig. And even you, Richard Nixon with an eye patch and horns. Please ask *why* I smoked. Ask what is happening to me and why I am changing. Then understand and perhaps, advise. Oh. I see. Were there drugs in the house? What kinds and how much?? Who gave who what?? Law and order. Definitely. Can you see that you're not interested in me anymore?? You only care for your mold for me—that mold that I cannot accept. And you hassle me out of love you say. You make me sick most of the time. You really don't understand.

Readers have, as a rule, had mixed responses to "Dilemma No. 9." Some are immediately sympathetic; others feel the paper is trite. To explain your own response, you might begin by considering either the narrator's personality or the form of the paper. The paper is written as an interior monologue; that is, it attempts to reproduce the writer's personal thoughts and feelings. This may be an unfamiliar style to some of you. Occasionally readers will tell me that this paper would not have been accepted in their high school composition classes. Others in my classes usually respond by arguing that it should have been. To support your opinion—whatever it may be—you will want to discuss the style, language, tone, point of view, and purpose of the paper—all of which lead back to the question of whether or not the paper is effective or successful writing.

What is the purpose of the paper? It was written as an auto-biographical sketch; but beyond that, what was the writer trying to communicate? One reader might say that the writer first is expressing her frustration and disgust with her parents and society, and finally is pleading for honest understanding. Another might say the paper is an exercise in self-pity—that the narrator wants understanding but is not willing to extend understanding to others. To support this, the reader could point out that the writer refuses to start a discussion with her parents and is unwilling to try to see things from their point of view; yet she expects them to see hers. Still another reader might say that the narrator's main purpose is simply to spill out miscellaneous thoughts and feelings as they cross her mind.

The title suggests that several confrontations similar to this one have occurred in the past, but the body of the paper makes no references to a pattern of repeated offenses on either the parents' or the daughter's part. As a result, some of you may feel that the narrator's parents are not unreasonable or lacking in understanding. You may suggest therefore that the writer offer more evidence of the parents' failure—perhaps some references to their preoccupation with their own problems, their double standards, their distortion of the truth, and so on, so that the daughter's attitude might be more explicitly justified.

Others of you may be disturbed because the writer assumes you share her views of the police and of smoking pot. Though you find her comments sincere, perhaps you do not sympathize with her opinions or attitudes. The description of Detective Ackerman's physical appearance, for example, helps demonstrate why the writer reacts as she does. Still, you may be annoyed that she so quickly labels him a pig. You may also point out that she assumes that her audience agrees when she disparages Ackerman for looking "like something out of a camping trip." More than one reader has noticed that the writer is guilty of the same fault she attributes to her parents—judging by appearances.

Other details in the paper may evoke positive response from you. The initial characterization of the parents is convincing: "Mother is giving me the back of her head under the ruse of peeling carrots and slamming dishes around," and "Dad, with a drink to stay his nerves, gazes through weary eyes from atop his lofty bar stool." The repeated references to *Time* magazine help unify the essay and signal that the narrator has returned to the immediate situation in the kitchen. ("Richard M. Nixon, I give you a pierced ear.") The continued defacement of Nixon's picture helps to underscore the writer's attack on establishment views.

Many of you may find the paper's style, organization, and

language effective. The single paragraph both unifies the paper and illustrates the continuousness of the writer's thoughts; paragraphing is not at all necessary in interior monologue. The mixture of colloquial slang and profane language also may be acceptable to you, since it is representative of the girl's private thoughts and language and thereby appropriate for the style of the paper.

Both the setting and the sequence of events in the paper are somewhat confusing. It is difficult to clearly distinguish what has happened before from what is happening now and to determine where it is happening. The writer does not structure her references to the fur coat, the Ann Arbor police, and her parents' behavior in a clearly defined chronology or setting. Later in the paper the writer jumps perhaps too abruptly from past to present, though the references to *Time* do help signal the switch.

What is perhaps most obvious in this paper is the writer's involvement in her subject. Whether or not you are sympathetic to her situation and attitude, many of you will agree that she *cares* about her subject. She is expressing opinions and feelings that are important to her.

Many of the papers written for a composition class can be considered "working papers," or papers in progress. The class discussion, then, is intended to give the writer ideas about what still needs to be done. There is no need for you to aggressively defend your paper or opinion in these discussions. At their best, class discussions are open forums in which you feel free to change your opinions and positions if and when you are convinced of another's point of view. The purpose of discussion is not to learn how to argue or how to "win points," but to examine papers and exchange views, however different they may be, and then perhaps to reassess your own views. If you are receptive to the views of others and are willing to offer your own, you are engaging in an experience that will provide you with insights into both the writing and the reading process.

I have emphasized that criticism should be constructive and supportive. There is no point in making unnecessarily derogatory remarks or strong, unsupported negative comments. They embarrass and humiliate a young writer, and they discourage discussion. To avoid later unpleasant and unproductive confrontations, your class might discuss what it feels the limits for negative comments should be. Certainly it is fair to ask the audience to offer some suggestions for improvement when they point out a paper's weaknesses. If they feel a paper is too vague or abstract, they might suggest specific kinds of details that could be included.

Being supportive in your criticism, however, is not the same as simply offering vague compliments. Though it is perfectly acceptable to open a discussion of a paper by saying it was amusing or fun to read, these responses are only a beginning. As a writer you may be temporarily satisfied with such responses, but they do not offer you much substantive assistance. If you are going to improve your writing skills, you will need more specific comments. Ordinarily, you will want to know why your paper is liked or disliked; you may want and need suggestions for improvement. When you get only vague or superficial responses, you may wonder if the class has read the paper carefully. Superficial comments may indicate the readers' indifference to a paper—their unwillingness to involve themselves in careful reading and discussion. When you spend a good deal of time and effort on a paper, you will be understandably disappointed if the audience brushes it aside with a few superficial remarks, even if they are complimentary.

There will be times, of course, when you are not interested in a given paper. Faked enthusiasm then would be pointless. There is little point in trying to fool yourself or the writer with compliments. But it is worth your time to determine *why* you are indifferent about a paper. What is missing? What would make the paper more interesting? By answering these questions not only do you examine your own tastes in writing, but you can offer constructive response to the writer.

Another problem may arise, particularly during the early part of a course when you are writing mainly about yourselves and your feelings. You may think that it is inappropriate to respond to or evaluate writing that is wholly subjective. If you do, this too is worth discussing in class, especially since the early assignments suggested in this book do emphasize personal perspective and experience. Remember, however, that a personal essay may be judged by different criteria than an expository essay; its purpose, manner, and audience will be different. As I said earlier, any piece of writing should be judged by its own premises and intent. In addition, it is important to distinguish between writing for yourself and writing for an audience. Writing intended for a personal journal, whose only audience is the individual writer, *is* perhaps exempt from outside criticism. But writing that is intended for any wider audience—a class, a publication, or the like—does open itself to responses from that audience. When you write a paper for a class, even a personal paper, you should care what your audience thinks about it. If you care about what you have written, you will care about whether it is understood and will want to know what has been misunderstood. If you want your audience to sympathize with you and they don't, you will probably decide to change some things to win their sympathy. Or if you are using dialogue and the class is confused about who is speaking, you will doubtless want to know that too. If the class reacts negatively to an incident that was intended to evoke a positive response, you will need to know what could be changed so that they will respond more positively. In other words, writing about yourself does not eliminate the need or importance of carefully examining and assessing that writing. Even in the realm of personal, subjective writing there are criteria you can use to decide that one paper is better and more successful than another or that some writing is not as effective or as successful as it might be.

As a reader you ought to be cautious about judging a paper on the basis of the writer's sincerity. A writer's personal sincerity does not guarantee a successful, interesting, or convincing paper. You must learn to distinguish the writer's personality in class and any announced purpose from what is actually written on the page. The two can be and often are connected, but sincerity in itself is not sufficient to produce a good paper. Though you should be aware of the writer's attitude, you must also exercise some degree of emotional detachment when you read. You must learn to distinguish what you think the writer is trying to say from what he or she is actually saying. When you can do this, you are then in a position to be more helpful in your responses.

Finally, it is important that you not confuse the writing skill with the opinion expressed by a writer. If you disagree with the opinion expressed in a paper, you can, of course, say so, but you should also indicate whether that opinion is clearly and convincingly expressed.

These introductory chapters have discussed some important ideas about language, writing, and the classroom writing situation. As you begin to explore the writing experiences suggested in the chapters that follow, you may find it helpful to refer to or reread these early chapters. They are offered not simply as in introduction but as a source of continuing support and assistance as you explore and experiment with writing in the weeks to come.

self encounter

Writing is a means of establishing your relationship to the world. In Chapter 1, I talked about words as a link—a medium through which you encounter the world and establish your relationship to it. Language enables you to discover, shape, interpret, and communicate your experience; in fact, it may even be considered as the very texture of experience. Words are the primary content of your life. Your existence is so immersed in language that words almost literally shape your life and make your reality.

For now, however, let's consider language in just one of its aspects: as a means of expressing and extending yourself. Writing about yourself is an especially complex and demanding process. First you must discover and interpret yourself—your inner thoughts, your emotional responses, your experience with the world. Then you must find a language and a form that captures and communicates your experience. These two activities—self-discovery and expression—are, of course, fundamental and continuing processes. You are continually exploring yourself and your experiences. But when you write about yourself, you are not only exploring and interpreting your inner life, you are also discovering language and relating to others.

Given the complexity of this task, you may find it difficult to know where to begin. The suggestions and discussion offered in this chapter are intended to stimulate—even, if necessary, to re-awaken—an awareness of your inner life and to lead you to discover a language and style that will express the individual quality of your experience.

You can begin by thinking of yourself as both subject and audience, in a relatively limited sense. Through your senses, for example, you become aware of both yourself and the world. You can feel your tense muscles, hear your stomach growl, and see your reflection in a mirror. You also encounter the world directly through sense impressions: the odor of burning candles, the texture of burlap, the sound of high heels striking pavement, the taste of cinnamon, the sight of newly plowed earth—these sensations suggest how you experience the world. Often what you feel and what you think are influenced by your sense impressions. The sound of a loud raspy voice may cause you to react negatively to a person, but the sound of a fire crackling in a fireplace may give you a feeling of security. The feel of wriggling worms may make you dislike fishing, but the texture of a baby's skin may please you. Undoubtedly, your sensual response to people and objects influences what you think about them.

When you were young, you were probably more directly aware of your sense impressions than you are now. As you grow older, some of these impressions become dulled. James Joyce begins *A Portrait of the Artist as a Young Man* by describing the sense impressions Stephen experienced as a baby—his father's hairy face, a song about wild rose blossoms, the warmth of a wet bedsheet, then its coldness and its queer smell. Later Stephen's sense impressions are combined with associations. The cold night air of the chapel reminds him of the cold of the sea and how cold and dark it was under the sea wall beside his father's house. In similar ways you also link associations with sense impressions. The scent of lavender may remind you of your grandmother; the creak of stairs may recall a frightening childhood incident; the touch of gravel on bare feet may remind you of your first summer at camp.

As a writer you want to become more aware—more conscious of the sense impressions you experience—so that you can communicate your experience more fully and genuinely. Through your senses the world grows more vividly alive for you and in turn you become more aware of yourself. The world you experience and the self you experience are unique. Through language you can more fully perceive your relationship to the world. Walt Whitman's poem "There Was a Child Went Forth" expresses just this kind of relationship.

THERE WAS A CHILD WENT FORTH

There was a child went forth every day,
And the first object he look'd upon, that object he became,
And that object became part of him for the day or a certain
    part of the day,
Or for many years or stretching cycles of years.

The early lilacs became part of this child,
And grass and white and red morning-glories, and white and
    red clover, and the song of the phoebe-bird,
And the Third-month lambs and the sow's pink-faint litter,
    and the mare's foal and the cow's calf,
And the noisy brood of the barnyard or by the mire of the
    pond-side,
And the fish suspending themselves so curiously below there,
    and the beautiful curious liquid,
And the water-plants with their graceful flat heads, all
    became part of him.

The field-sprouts of Fourth-month and Fifth-month became
    part of him,
Winter-grain sprouts and those of the light-yellow corn,
    and the esculent roots of the garden,
And the apple-trees cover'd with blossoms and the fruit
    afterward, and wood-berries, and the commonest weeds by
    the road,
And the old drunkard staggering home from the outhouse of
    the tavern whence he had lately risen,
And the schoolmistress that pass'd on her way to the school,
And the friendly boys that pass'd, and the quarrelsome boys,
And the tidy and fresh-cheek'd girls, and the barefoot negro
    boy and girl,
And all the changes of city and country wherever he went.

His own parents, he that had father'd him and she that had
    conceiv'd him in her womb and birth'd him,
They gave this child more of themselves than that,
They gave him afterward every day, they became part of him.

The mother at home quietly placing the dishes on the
supper-table,
The mother with mild words, clean her cap and gown, a
wholesome odor falling off her person and clothes as
she walks by,
The father, strong, self-sufficient, manly, mean, anger'd,
unjust,
The blow, the quick loud word, the tight bargain, the crafty
lure,
The family usages, the language, the company, the furniture,
the yearning and swelling heart,
Affection that will not be gainsay'd, the sense of what is
real, the thought if after all it should prove unreal,
The doubts of day-time and the doubts of night-time, the
curious whether and how,
Whether that which appears so is so, or is it all flashes
and specks?
Men and women crowding fast in the streets, if they are not
flashes and specks what are they?
The streets themselves and the facades of houses, and goods
in the windows,
Vehicles, teams,the heavy-plank'd wharves, the huge crossing
at the ferries,
The village on the highland seen from afar at sunset, the
river between,
Shadows, aureola and mist, the light falling on roofs and
gables of white or brown two miles off,
The schooner near by sleepily dropping down the tide, the
little boat slack-tow'd astern,
The hurrying tumbling waves, quick-broken crests, slapping,
The strata of color'd clouds, the long bar of maroon-tint
away solitary by itself, the spread of purity it lies
motionless in,
The horizon'd edge, the flying sea-crow, the fragrance of
salt marsh and shore mud,
These became part of that child who went forth every day,
and who now goes, and will also go forth every day.

The child's going forth is presented in concrete, sensuous details.
His growth is expressed by the increasing diversity and complexity
in what he encounters as he goes forth. As his experiences expand,

so do his perceptions, and they all become part of him: he assimilates the world he sees and accommodates himself to it.

You too can discover and express the ways you experience the world by recording your sense impressions in writing. You might, for example, try to list all the sense impressions you experience in a given place for a specific length of time. Perhaps you can spend fifteen or twenty minutes sitting under a tree, in the lobby of the library, in the dining room of the dormitory, or on a park bench. Pay attention to what you hear, taste, touch, and smell. Ignore visual impressions at first, since they are so readily accessible. How does the grass feel under your legs? Can you smell the odor of cigarettes? of flowers? of food? Can you hear automobiles? insects buzzing? papers rattling? phones ringing? What about taste sensations? Can you taste your lips, the pen you are using, the cold night air, the aftertaste of cigarettes, the sweetness of gum? Most of us habitually restrict our senses. When we deliberately open ourselves to the world around us, it is amazing how many sensations bombard us. Here is what one student recorded during a twenty-minute period:

I hear the sound of a fingernail file rasping over nails.

I see the flickering light of the candle flame, as well as watch the wax dripping down the candle side and finally hardening near the bottom into a small ball.

I hear the click as the record player is turned on as well as the music which follows.

I hear the turning of pages in the book my girlfriend is studying, and the squeak as her hi-lighter goes across the page.

The voices of visitors in the room, and the sound of the door closing as they leave.

I hear the ticking of the four alarm clocks in our suite.

I hear the large flakes of snow hitting the window and melting.

I hear the key turn in the door as I leave.

I see, hear, and smell popcorn popping.

I hear the slow, oily sort of sound as the elevator door closes and opens.

I listen to the money dropping into the vending machines and the noises made as the food drops into the tray.

I taste the tingling carbonated drink.

I sense the cold fingers which result from carrying a glass of cold soda up six flights of stairs.

I see the windows frosting up.

My feet scruff across the dirty rug, several threads are pulled out of it.

I see and hear the match ignited, watch as it ignites the stick of sealing wax. I watch the drops as wax falls on the paper, and smell the match as it goes out.

I watch my other roommates studying.

The light from the desk lamp hurts your eyes.

I see the little droplets of orange pop clinging to the sides of the transparent plastic cup.

I see the lights of Hubbard and Akers Halls shining out in the dark.

I see my girlfriend nervously kicking her leg as she talks to a boy who is visiting in our room.

I notice the WED. stamp on my hand from the ice skating rink last night.

I hear a knock at the door.

I notice the venetian blind cords waving in the breeze from the open window.

I hear the faucet being turned on in the bathroom.

Though this writer does not consistently render the sensations in detail, she is beginning to discover the way words can express her sensual awareness of the world—the way they can make her more aware of her feelings. You might try to render your sense impressions even more directly and specifically in the following way:

Ticking of a clock
Muffled giggles
Cold bare feet wriggle on a smooth tile floor
Strong and bitter taste of tea trickles through my throat
Fuzzy pink watchbird watching me
Oh hell. I'm thinking poetry
Art it's not but merely rhyme
Anything to pass the time

Cold wind blowing through my toes
Hot tea's steam on my nose
The mug sounds scratch on the desk top
A horn sounds above traffic's roars
People laughing out-of-doors
Roommate choking as she pores
   over her assignment
Hard wood now against my heels
Laughter once more merrily peals
   this time from the room beyond
A smell of oranges wafting through
A door creaks shut and latches
The wastebasket needs emptying
Mournful stares from a yellow cat
Heat from a register on my back—contrast to the toes
Chair beneath me slipping fast
Heat now on my neck
Now on floor, cold and hard
Toe joints crack
Something pounds on the ceiling
Hollow scratching against wood
Pink and green together with orange
The gray ape stares from the door
   words surround him—cage him as in a zoo
Smoothness of paper, curling of hand,
Slippery purple pencil
Cool hard wire spiral
Writer's cramp

Although this is little more than a list, it is effective because it records a rich variety of sensuous detail. The writer is exploring and expressing how she experiences the world. The list also provides the writer with a beginning for other ways of communicating her experience. You may choose to begin another way—perhaps by recording sense impressions in a paragraph or in a more consistently rhymed pattern.

Another way you can record your immediate experience with the world is to communicate one specific sense impression in detail, like the texture of peanut butter:

PEANUT BUTTER

The glob of peanut butter lodges itself on the roof of my mouth. As it infiltrates my palate, it clings to each and every crevice. Similar to quicksand the glob seems to deceivingly invite the curious tongue. Then, when the victim is within reach, it sucks it into its overpowering depths. Slowly the sticky substance spreads like hot lava running down a mountain side. As the peanut butter enters the throat area a sickly feeling of choking pervades. Like someone filling a hole in the pavement with cement, the glob envelops the throat. As the saliva tries to cut at the strength, the peanut butter escapes and spreads itself thinly over teeth and gums. And the tongue battles to disperse the parasite, but the substance only oozes deeper and deeper until the slime-coated mouth waters uncontrollably in desperation to rid itself of the lingering aftertaste.

Or perhaps you could describe a particular sound:

THE SOUND OF A TOILET FLUSHING

When the mechanism is initially triggered, I hear the sound of a sudden turbulence of water, as though it is caught in a vacuum. Then there is silence for a split second, then the vacuum seemingly is released, and I hear the roaring, gurgling water, gallons of it falling but to a bottomless pit. Then suddenly there is a low gurgle, and water splashing against water, as if over a fall. A high pitched hiss, quite like that of steam escaping through a valve is the next sound. Suddenly it is stiller, except for a belchy groan. Then a high whiny sound, gradually diminishing, a sort of shush, and finally all is quiet.

These descriptions are, of course, exaggerated and somewhat strained. Nevertheless, such writing experience is valuable, for the writer not only has to focus on a detailed sense impression but also must find words that concretely communicate that impression. The major challenge here is to select appropriate and precise language. When you focus on one concrete sensation, you become acutely aware of the importance and necessity of choosing clear and exact language.

Direct sense impressions often lead beyond themselves to emotional responses or mental associations. When you hear a cat meowing, what do you think or feel? Does the odor of pipe tobacco remind you of anything? Not all our sense impressions stimulate associations or responses, but it is surely worth recording those associations you do have. In doing so you may become more conscious of the patterns of mental and emotional images you have developed, and you may also become more conscious of the uniqueness of your interactions with the world. When you search for words to capture and communicate your experience, you discover too that language is the medium through which you clarify and communicate your uniqueness. Undoubtedly there have been times when you have observed or sensed things that evoked strong responses from you. Because your mind processes information so rapidly, you may not have been conscious of what initiated your response. By recording specific sensations and the associations they evoke, you can more clearly distinguish the process by which you perceive and experience the world. Notice how the writers in the examples below link each sense impression with an association.

SENSE IMPRESSIONS

A far off train whistle is a lonely sound, taking someone away or leaving me behind.

The wind is blowing and rattling the leaves. The wind is always there, the only thing that changes is its personality.

The leaves are brittle and crunchy when I scuffle through them, the trees' fresh garbage.

The smell of popcorn comes down the hall, warm, inviting, friends together.

Natural science book left open to astronomy, the universe, what's outside, if it has an outside?

Brushes jammed in a glass jar, thick and then light makes the brushes dance inside.

41

The drinking fountain gurgles and echoes in the hall. You have to bend low in high school, but on tiptoe in the grades.

Silver piggy stands on the desk; blank, expressionless face tries to hide emptiness.

In the night someone runs past our window, like two clapping hands quick and steady.

Window hung apples stay cold and hard. Halloween is coming, reaching with a too small mouth for apples, then freezing in a mothermade clown suit.

In my hand soft charcoal and a piece of paper, blend it into the fibers with finger tips, make the flat round.

SENSE IMPRESSIONS WITH ASSOCIATIONS

I hear the sharp thud of someone kicking a football. It reminds me of being at a football game, the rumble of the crowd ooing as one, after a well-kicked ball.

I smell a pile of dried leaves burning. As I walk through the thick, gray smoke, I want to run, to let go, to unleash myself from the chains of custom and habit.

I see a girl with a brown skirt and brown sweater, except with yellow and red and orange mixed in. She looks like fallen autumn leaves, so pretty you don't want to burn them.

I feel the dry leaves crumble under my bare feet. It reminds me of ". . . and unto dust shalt thou return."

I taste the piercing flavor of a cold red apple. I remember all the football games where I've eaten apples and also my grandmother's apple pies.

I see a guy and a girl walking, crunching the dry leaves as they wander hand in hand, swishing their feet through the leaves. It reminds me of the times I've just walked through all the brown and color, and thought.

There's a bell-like clarity in the air I smell. I've smelled its crisp cleanness before. The air smells so bright and clean because the loitering, lived-in summer air is being swept away by the cool north wind.

I see people moving, a panorama of color. I can't remember ever seeing people standing still on a breezy fall day. They seem to move with the wind.

I feel the luscious first snowflake melt on the tip of my tongue. It reminds me of the coming winter and the short cold days ahead.

I look up and see the ominous steel-gray clouds hanging low in the sky. It seems like a good time to light the fire.

Exercises like these encourage writers to develop a concrete personal style. Notice the writer's use of detail in the second example. The writing does have weaknesses: some sentences are poorly constructed ("I see a girl with a brown skirt and brown sweater, except with yellow and red and orange mixed in"); others are ambiguous ("I remember all the football games where I've eaten apples and also my grandmother's apple pies"). But the writer also includes some sharply vivid images, like the "piercing flavor of a cold red apple" and the "loitering, lived-in summer air." Much of the language is personal and precise. As an audience we are able to share the writer's sensations and enter into his mental and emotional experience.

Linking sense impressions with emotional or mental associations is one way to explore your inner life. There are other kinds of writing experiences, too, that will help you discover a language to embody your personal, subjective life. Each of us has a complex and continuous interior language. This constantly flowing internal stream of words, phrases, images, and ideas is a rich source of language for writing. The written record of our interior language is called *interior monologue* or *stream of consciousness*. In an interior monologue the writer reproduces thoughts and feelings in a way that suggests this stream. There is no need consciously to shape or organize the writing, though the finished paper may in fact have some kind of organic structure. Many modern works of fiction include stream of consciousness writing and, of course, these writings are consciously shaped. One of the more famous examples is the final chapter of James Joyce's *Ulysses*. The entire chapter is a record of Molly Bloom's thoughts as she lies in bed at night, remembering and imagining. Joyce uses no punctuation in this passage, which emphasizes the free flowing character of Molly's reflections.

Yes because he never did a thing like that before as ask to get his breakfast in bed with a couple of eggs since the *City Arms* hotel when he used to be pretending to be laid up with a sick voice doing his highness to make himself interesting to that old faggot Mrs. Riordan that he thought he had a great leg of and she never left us a farthing all for masses for herself and her soul greatest miser ever was actually afraid to lay out 4d for her methylated spirit telling me all her ailments she had too much old chat in her about politics and earthquakes and the end of the world let us have a bit of fun first God help the world if all the women were her sort down on bathing suits and lownecks of course nobody wanted her to wear I suppose she was pious because no man would look at her twice I hope I'll never be like her . . . .

Molly's inner language may not be similar to yours, but the selection does illustrate the rich stream of inner language that flows through the human mind. Your inner language may be disorganized and fragmented, but it can reveal your private experience, and it can provide a valuable source for expressing yourself in writing.

Another way of tapping your inner language is by writing free associations. You can begin by selecting an object, preferably one to which you have no particular emotional attachment. Then in a limited period of time—ten or fifteen minutes—record all the ideas, sense impressions, or emotional reactions the object elicits. The following free association is in response to a clock and was written by an individual who had never done a free association before.

FREE ASSOCIATION—CLOCK

45 minutes of class left
A clock wakes me in the morning
Time goes by so fast

Seems late before it's even been early
Clocks are all shapes and sizes
Mine is white and the alarm buzzes
Dislike the alarm to go off in the morning
Especially if I didn't go to bed until late—like last night
Some clocks tick loud
And most alarms sound different
My alarm goes off 30 minutes later than what it is set for
I'm tired, can't think fast enough
We gave a clock like that one to my cousin for his high
    school graduation
Doesn't help him any—he's always late anyhow
Clocks-Hickory Dickory Dock the mouse ran up and down
    the clock
Cinderella didn't need a clock to tell her what time it was
Grandfather clocks, I wonder where they got their name
My Grandfather's clock was little and hung on the wall in his
    den
Time, I remember watching the clock waiting for my first
    date, my first formal, my first class
Time, there's never enough of it

When you write free associations, you may discover language that expresses the rich variety of your inner emotional and mental activity. In the example above the writer mixes concrete references to time in her immediate classroom and campus situation with references to time in her past. She also includes a few abstract references to time. The first half of the association is more restricted to her immediate existence, but in the second half she begins to draw on a wider variety of her ideas and experiences with time.

If you enjoy doing free associations, you could write one and then revise it to make the language more vivid and concrete. Notice how detailed and specific many of the images are in this revised free association on a bottle of pills:

PILLS

Winter cold misery—stuffy nose, watery eyes, crumpled Kleenex.

Lying on wrinkled linens trying to remain on one side to keep one nostril clear of congestion.

Remember the allergy I made up? All about flowers. I faked sneezes, doctor prescribed green pills, carried them around, fooled them—made it all up.

Sickness in the hospital—a green one—a big white one in a paper cup at 11:30 every night.

Blue pills the color of my new skirt.

My doll hospital with all the torn up dolls we tried to mend.

Necco candy—the chocolate are the best. But red M&M's are even better.

Birth control—Elaine—we were such good friends once— wow—she's pregnant now—my age and having a baby has to get married—sweet Elaine. She was such a nice girl.

A diet pill—kept me up all night—dry mouth so nervous.

Mescaline—Doug, I knew Doug. He overdosed on a pill— "flipped out" freaky—crazy Doug.

Marty the dirty-minded druggist. Marc, my old boyfriend worked for him and related to me the dirty stories he told.

A bottle of aspirin—took 5—chickened out—so long ago.

A big red and black capsule so hard to swallow with a sore throat.

105° temperature—delirious—toothpick soldiers marching outside my window, the moving bed.

A shot—hate shots.

The Naked Lunch worst book I ever read, William Burroughs had to be perverted not only a junkie.

Valley of the Dolls—dad got mad when he found me reading it.

Status—every one in school carried some kind of pills around.

Array of colors, shapes, and sizes. How does the doctor know which one to give for what?

One pill makes you larger
One pill makes you small
And the ones that mother gives you don't do
    anything at all
Go ask Alice when she's ten feet tall

        "White Rabbit," Jefferson Airplane [1]

Once I saw a Tab of LSD—in my art class at home. I didn't believe something so small could cause something so big.

Placebo—Mrs. Janis's Freudian outlook in our psyc. class.

Grandma died. Not all the pills in the world could save her and her wet kisses. I blamed God for her death—I was only five.

Down, down, down the stomach through.

Excedrin headaches, Bromo Seltzer stomach aches, Bayer hangovers, American society.

Commercials—everyone is sick—Can Susie com' out an' pway??

Two aspirin—The cure-all of a civilization.

We learn a good deal about the writer in this selection. She relates experiences from her youth—her doll hospital and her grandmother's death. We also learn about her friends, her high school experiences, her attitudes about American life; we even learn that she once considered suicide. And all this is expressed in graphic and concrete language.

    Once you have explored your inner language and recorded it in free forms such as interior monologue and free association, you might try to focus on one or two specific experiences, exploring them in greater detail. Communicating your thoughts and emotions in a controlled manner is a challenging task. First you must be aware of what you think or feel; then you must consciously work to develop a style, a language, and a tone that best communicate those thoughts or feelings.

You might begin by considering your emotions. Try to be specific and concrete when you write about them because the abstract terms that refer to emotions —*love, hate, fear, disgust, pity*— do not mean the same things to everyone. Each of us experiences these emotions in a unique way. Though you will not always want or need to communicate your emotional responses in detail, it is well worth the effort to try to convey them concretely. By doing so you may find a language to communicate a depth, intensity, and personal dimension that are lacking when you simply label your emotions. By closely examining your emotional reactions to the world you are forced once again to become aware of the specific details and personal nature of these reactions. And once again you will see the importance of selecting suitable language.

Do you know what is meant when a writer says he or she is angry? In a general sense, of course, you do know that the writer is experiencing extreme displeasure. You also know how you feel when *you* are angry. But until a writer specifically conveys *his* or *her* personal experience, you really do not know how that writer experiences anger. Your challenge as a writer is to find language that will personally, clearly, and precisely communicate your emotions. How do you feel when you are angry? How does your body react? What kind of gestures or actions typically express your anger? What do you think about when you are angry? Can you find a metaphor that would appropriately communicate your anger? Do you experience different kinds of anger? Can you articulate the difference? These are the kinds of questions you should ask yourself when you are writing about your emotions. The questions require you, of course, to gain some objectivity about your emotional responses and also encourage you to become more aware of what emotions you experience.

Here is how one freshman girl described fear:

FEAR

Slowly, my eyes open and remain riveted on a point above my head. A slight shiver runs up and down my stiffened spine, even though I am covered by a sheet. Imaginary, ghostlike hands keep me from moving around. My sensitive ears strain to perceive every unusual noise, a creak in the hall, an owl with his mournful wail, the cool night breeze rustling the curtains at my open window, the ticking of the clock grows louder and louder until the whole room seems to be echoing the words, "Beware, beware." Beads of perspiration trickle down my face, leaving in their wake imaginary tears. Cold waves of anxiety clutch at my stomach, causing me to feel sick and faint. A certain numbness sneaks up on me, until my whole body tingles within its grasp. I am afraid . . .

In the next excerpt a student describes tension.

TENSION

My heart thumps wildly. It vibrates soundly against my chest. Eyes scanning the drab wall, they eventually search the face of a clock which ticks noisily and grates on my ears sharply. I stand rigidly and suddenly pace the floor in my short, choppy steps, my shoes clacking along the polished floor in rhythm with the unceasing tick-tock of the clock. Distraught, I flop into a chair with a sigh, seeking peace within myself. The tension will not end: My hands fly to my lips and my teeth open like the hungry fangs of a tiger, waiting to rip its prey to shreds. I tear into the fingernails fiercely, chewing, biting, unable to stop, wanting desperately to stop. A knock sounds on my door. I start, then jump out of my chair and hurry, in a state of disorder, to the door. Anxiety clouds my perception. I can neither see nor hear the person in front of me. My head spins. It flees from itself to escape the pressure but can find no refuge. One palm brushes another, wet with perspiration, cold and clammy. My hands quickly grab a piece of the newspaper and begin snatching pieces from it, nervously, the rustle of paper momentarily overshadowing a deep pounding of the heart. I can barely feel the inside of my mouth, dry, parched, as if left by the desert sun to shrivel away. Cold sweat beads upon my forehead. Teasing butterflies unsettle my stomach, playfully darting from one corner to another as I tap on the edge of my desk with a pencil. Sighs breeze through my lips in quick succession; I breathe heavily. There are no nails left to chew, only the cuticles. I twirl a finger through my hair tensely. And the clock continues to tick incessantly, driving me almost insane with anxiety.

Like the descriptions of a specific sense impression, both selections here are exaggerated. You would seldom describe your emotions in such a detailed manner, but the writing experience does allow you to find words that express emotion in concrete ways.

The writing discussed so far focuses primarily on the immediate encounters between yourself and the world. But exploration of the self need not deal only with the way you presently respond and feel. You can also write about your memories, for you have been shaped and influenced by your past. Your memories hold both the experience and the language to help you communicate your present self.

It is sometimes difficult to remember childhood experiences. They are often buried deep in our memories and recur only in fragments. Some experiences you may not wish to recall; those you can allow to remain dormant. You may want to revive other memories, however, that are presently fragmented or vague. You could begin by listing some objects or images from your childhood and linking them to specific memories.

IMAGES OF CHILDHOOD

smells—the first day of school had a smell

fights—my sister and I in constant battle

accidents—going to the hospital so many times I knew the emergency ward by heart

onions—always ate whole onions and never had a cold

pictures—my dad constantly taking pictures of the family

eating—I never stopped. I was the fattest kid around

swing set—my sister told me to jump, so I did. I fractured my arm.

bicycle—falling over in a mud puddle, learning to ride without training wheels.

snow—making angels and playing Fox and Geese

croquet—Hitting a kid in the head with a mallet

Christmas—getting up at 5:30 and told to go back to bed

An exercise like this one helps open the doors to language and experience. It also helps you to communicate specific information rather than general information about your happy or unhappy childhood.

Another possible writing exercise involves recalling and recording unrelated incidents. In each of the following examples the writers move randomly from one set of memories to the next.

IMAGES OF CHILDHOOD

Childhood—my dog oh how I loved that dog. I used
to call him Hot Dog because he looked just like one. I
ran away with him to the hospital and my mom got worried
and called the police. Hot Dog got killed by a car. I cried
all day.

The tricycle—I shouldn't have hurt the little boy on the
tricycle. I don't why why I did it.

Sitting next door watching my dad chase my little sister
around the backyard trying to catch her and put
her diaper back on.

Got caught stealing baseball cards from the drugstore.
Mom didn't do anything. I was lucky.

Fifth grade—in love for the first time, but she liked somebody
else better—so sad.

Smoke-filled house. Started a fire in the fireplace, forgot to
open the latch, everybody running out of the house for air.

Little League baseball and football were great because
I was always the star. Proud of my dad-coach of the
Detroit Lions football team, love the attention.

Funeral—father dies, so sad, didn't cry though—
don't know why I didn't.

Sitting in a chair and never being able to touch the floor with your feet, always wondering when you are going to be old enough to be in "high school," snowballs, cotton candy.

Searching behind the old sofa for your Easter basket because you knew that was a good place, getting up in the wee hours of Christmas morning and almost knocking over the Christmas tree in the dark and then running into the parents' room and screaming that there was a burglar in the living room trying to steal the presents.

Standing on the kitchen cabinet with a dozen eggs intent on killing the first brother that came through the swinging door; if it's a kick at the door, aim low because it's a smaller brother; if it's a silent push aim high because it's a tall, older brother.

Spacemen, army men, conniving constantly for a shiny quarter, always laughing, never working, always with the gang. Hey, you guys, *Wizard of Oz* is on tonight. Aw, shutup, your mother's a man.

These writing experiences are valuable because they probe your memories and encourage you to recall particulars of isolated incidents. As you record them, you should keep in mind the importance of selecting precise language.

This chapter has encouraged you to explore your intimate life. Writing about your private thoughts and experiences is valuable for several reasons. Initially, it makes you more alert to your responses to the world. By stating these responses as well as feeling them, you can discover a language that will intensify and give a design and meaning to them. Examining your immediate responses also may help you to clarify your perceptions and sensitivity to the world.

When you write about yourself, you are using language to perceive and express your life and to extend yourself to others. The writing that deals with your immediate mental and emotional encounters with yourself and the world is perhaps the most personal and private writing you do. It often involves little or no distance between writer, audience, and subject. Such writing is best suited to free forms or modes.

These free forms are especially appropriate as journal entries written to and for yourself only. In journals you can record your most private and intimate experiences. Though some journals may be addressed to a small, intimate audience, as a rule, journal writing involves the least distance between self, audience, and subject. You may choose to record some of your early attempts at stream of consciousness writing, free association, or other types of personal explorations in your journal. Later you will perhaps select or revise some entries to present to the class.

When you write for an audience other than yourself, you need to consider that audience. Writing about your emotions and sensations should not be equated with impressionistic or sentimental, self-indulgent writing that makes no attempt to communicate clearly. It is not enough to say simply, "Here is how I feel. *I* understand it, and that is enough." Writers have an obligation to express their feelings and ideas clearly to an audience. If you care about what you write, you will also want it to be understood. As a writer you need response from an audience; as an audience you are obligated to give honest, helpful feedback. Exchanges between writers and audience in the classroom should emphasize the need for concrete expression of your emotions and thoughts. Your audience may not, for example, experience fear or joy in the same way you do.

Writing about the self is an important beginning. Being in touch with yourself will enable you to examine more clearly the region beyond you. Yet it is also important to remember that writing that concentrates primarily or exclusively on the self as subject or the self as audience is limited both in perception and perspective. The writing experiences included in this chapter are intended only as ways to begin. To more fully understand yourself and your world you must emerge from self-absorption and examine and express your relationship to places, to other people, and to your social institutions.

APPROPRIATE WRITING MODES

Before I list some specific writing assignments for this chapter, it might be helpful first to summarize several modes that are especially appropriate for writing about the self. Subjective writing, you will remember, best lends itself to open or free forms that allow the writer a good deal of freedom. The modes reviewed here are meant only to suggest possible approaches to writing about the self.

interior monologue

An interior monologue is a written record of our inner thoughts, emotions, and reactions. Sometimes this is called stream of consciousness or stream of reflection writing. It attempts to capture and record the flow of thought and feeling that we experience at any given period of time: the writer simply records thoughts on paper. Many times these thoughts are so personal that the individual records them in a journal only; at other times this kind of writing can be consciously organized for an audience. "Dilemma No. 9" (p. 25) is an example of an interior monologue written for a class. For a professional example of this kind of writing you may wish to look at the final chapter of James Joyce's *Ulysses*. Sometimes interior monologue assumes a shape of its own that gives it meaning (as in *Ulysses*). Such a shape may develop from recurring images, feelings, or thoughts. (The writer's use of *Time* magazine helps to shape "Dilemma 9.") Often, however, this kind of writing will be relatively shapeless. In any event it is a legitimate way of beginning to know and express yourself.

immediate responses

These are extemporaneously written responses to a specific stimulus. The response may be written in prose, poetry, list form, or any other form you choose. The stimulus might be a film, a photograph, a painting, an article read aloud in class, a specific object in the classroom, a demonstration (perhaps staged by the teacher or another student), or any other object or activity you select. The procedure is quite simple. After seeing a film, hearing a poem, or looking at an object, for example, you write down your immediate response to that stimulus.

One specific kind of immediate response is a *free association*. Here you or the teacher selects a specific object (a pen, a paper cup, a set of keys, a watch, and the like) as a stimulus. Then in a given time period you record all the ideas, emotions, or responses evoked by that object. Each individual response should be linked to the object. The writing can be in list or paragraph form. Later you may want to record a free association on abstract ideas, such as love, hate, jealousy, and so on. (For an example of free association see p. 44.)

Immediate responses often assume a shape that gives them added meaning, but no particular structure or organization is required. The intent is to allow you to express yourself openly and to examine how your mind and emotions respond to specific situations.

sense impressions

Sense impressions are a written record of all the sensations experienced by a person at a particular time in a particular place. You record (in any form you wish) all you smell, taste, feel, hear, and see in that situation. Although our senses of sight and hearing usually dominate our impressions of the world, we need to give attention to all the senses to make our perceptions more complete; a total sense response is needed to fully experience the world.

free writing and other kinds of responses

Because free writing really has no limits in form or subject matter, you may write in any form about any topic. This writing might overlap some of the previous suggestions; that is, free writing can and does include interior monologue, immediate responses, and sense impressions, but it encompasses more than these too. You might describe the classroom or dramatize what you see outside; you might tell a story or a joke, write a letter to the class, or you might choose to play the role of a fictional character. The possibilities are nearly inexhaustible.

At times, responses other than written ones are possible. You may choose to explore and express yourself in a series of drawings, photographs, or paintings; perhaps you will decide to record some sounds that represent your life, compose a song, or construct a three-dimensional sculpture. You could bring to class an object that you feel in some way represents yourself. Such responses are valid ways to express ourselves; and they often provide the stimulus for other writing experiences.

journals

Any of the previous modes can be recorded in a journal. Journal writing is the most intimate of all the subjective modes. In a journal you can record your private thoughts, emotions, experiences, and questions. A journal can, in fact, be a record of your personal history. It objectifies the monologue we all carry within ourselves. By writing in a journal we can begin to see, capture, connect, and comprehend ourselves and our world. It can help us to find a language to express and communicate our inwardness or our encounters with the external world. Finally, as a record of our personal experiences and growth, a journal can provide us with raw material for later writing.

SPECIFIC WRITING POSSIBILITIES

Free Association.   In a specific time limit write down all the associations you have when you see a particular object. The object may be of your own choosing or it may be brought to class by the teacher.

Sense Impressions.   Spend ten or twenty minutes in a particular place recording all the sense impressions you experience there. Or as an alternative try to record all the sense impressions you recall from childhood. These can be done in list form or in paragraph form.

Select one sense impression and record it in as much detail as possible (that is, the sound of rain, the texture of a pen, the taste of gum, the odor of a cigar, and so on).

List a series of sense impressions along with the intellectual reflection or emotional association that the sensation evokes.

Describe what happens to your mind and/or your body when you experience a specific emotion, such as fear, joy, anxiety, loneliness, anticipation, and so on.

Recreate a circumstance in which you experienced an intense emotion. You might also want to demonstrate how your temperament or your opinions have been affected by that experience.

Identify a strong emotion or prejudice you have; then relate a particular incident that you feel caused it or contributed to it.

Describe a moment of insecurity or unpleasantness that you feel has contributed to your growth.

interactions
with
place

In the previous chapter we explored self as an initial topic for your writing. In this chapter you will be considering place as a writing topic, for exploration of place can be viewed as a natural movement outward from self. The well-known Swiss psychologist Jean Piaget has suggested that a child's growth develops outward from the self. During this process, which Piaget calls *decentering,* the self enlarges, assimilating the world to itself and accommodating itself to the world. The child in Whitman's poem (p. 35) experiences just this kind of assimilation and accommodation, and in a very real sense the child's development parallels our own growth. As our lives, for example, expand outward from self, we become increasingly aware of place. First, perhaps, we become aware of our immediate location—the room around us, the texture of the rug, the color of the drapes, the odor of the bouquet of flowers on a nearby table, the yard outside. As we continue to grow, we encounter place in an ever expanding and complex series of experiences. We move from our homes to a neighborhood, to cities, to distant vacation cottages, and perhaps we take trips abroad. And, like Whitman's child "going forth," we perceive ever increasing diversity and complexity in the elements that constitute a place; places become intricately entwined with people and events. The places we have lived in, visited, or imagined may substantially shape our lives. Place can influence our beliefs, our tastes and perspectives, and our behavior. Our views of family life, for example, are greatly influenced by the kind of place our home was. Similarly, our attitude toward public education may be shaped by what kind of place school was for us. Our conception of vacation is influenced by the places we have visited while on vacation. In these ways place helps to define us. In another sense our relationship to place is a transactional one, for we also help to shape place. Our perspectives and previous knowledge shape our view of a place. We can attribute meaning to a place, associate emotions with it, and assign certain modes of behavior to it. We might also respond imaginatively to a place. The meaning of a place can extend beyond its physical location: your subjective response also contributes to its meaning.

Each of us will experience place in our own unique manner. I will not perceive the Grand Canyon in quite the same way you will. Each of us will bring our own personal perspective, which will interpret that natural wonder for us, and each of us in turn will have our perspectives altered by the canyon. I may notice the subtle shadings of colors and the geographical patterns cut out by the cliffs; I may imagine the loneliness of someone lost in the vast maze of rock formations. My view both interprets the canyon and attributes meaning to it. What happens to me while I am there—my activities, my perceptions, and my encounters—will in turn add meaning to my life. The canyon may, for example, contribute to my understanding of loneliness. You, however, may view the canyon differently. Perhaps you will notice the sound of the roaring Colorado or the texture of the cliffs; you may imagine the exhilaration of the early explorers who successfully maneuvered the rapids. You will be influenced not by the loneliness of the canyon but by the challenge and adventure of it. It is in this interchange between you and place that a place becomes a situation. A city, a vacant lot, a prison cell, a snow-capped mountain, or a local drugstore each can become a situation—encompassing both a place and a person. Place as a situation is thus much more than a geographical location; it includes your personal interaction with that physical location.

You can write about place in a variety of styles and approaches. Perhaps the most familiar approach is a description of the physical characteristics of a geographical location. Often such a description will emphasize sense impressions.

It was eight o'clock on a Saturday morning. The sky was a clear blue and the summer sun brought a quiet light to the city once again. The large trees surrounding our house filtered most of the sun's light from the house. The resulting shadows contrasted sharply with the yard where the sun cast its light. The trees in the darkness of shadow were a deep, damp green. In the streets, stillness filled the air, as few people were about yet.

In these few sentences the writer establishes a setting and tone for his paper. It is also possible to emphasize more strongly the interpretation and imaginative response to a specific location.

The sleek canoe slithered like a shadow across the glassy lake toward a distant amber glow. Surrounding us on every side were the great, imposing Norway pines of Grand Taquamenon National Forest. Moving in peaceful tranquility across the water, my senses were awakened to sounds which had been completely foreign to me only the day before: the lonesome, eerie call of the loon; the croaking of bullfrogs lamenting the fact that their privacy had been invaded; the hooting of an owl; a paddle making contact with the water; the warning splash of a beaver. Silhouetted by moonlight at the stern of the canoe was the outlined form of my husband, the great white hunter, dressed in old bluejeans and sweatshirt, a cowboy hat on his head, and his .44 magnum pistol strapped around his waist, our only protection against this untamed, uncivilized wilderness.

Notice how the sense impressions in this passage are modified to contribute to the overall tone—"*eerie* call of the loon; the croaking of bullfrogs *lamenting* . . . the *warning* splash of a beaver." By using these interpretive adjectives the writer not only describes the lake but also communicates her emotional response to it.

We have already mentioned that for most of us a place consists of much more than a geographical location. The people who are there as well as the activities or events that occur there shape our concept of a place. It is possible, in fact, to characterize a place by quoting the conversations of people who are interacting there. Notice how, with a minimum of dialogue—and only dialogue—the following student paper captures the atmosphere of a bar.

"Play B-7."
"Ordering."
"Say, baby—wha' 'cha doin' tonight?"
"Turn that mother up."
"Ordering."
"Gimmie a couple of Bud's, will ya' Alfie?"
"Damn, it's cold outside."
"Anybody wanna play pool?"
"God, I hate Mondays."
"Listen honey, can I buy you a drink?"
"ORDERING!!!"
"Get your goddamn hands off me."
"Hey, Alfie, turn that thing down, I can't hear myself think."
"The freeways are so crowded after work."
"My wife'll kill me for this."
"I wanna zombie."
"$2.90."
"ORDERING!!!"

By the end of this brief series of comments we know something about the people, the encounters, the activities, the tone of the bar. The writer has been highly selective in her choice of dialogue and as a result the paper efficiently communicates a sense of the place.

Writing about a city, with its diversity and complexity, is an especially challenging task. One effective approach is to focus on an assortment of scenes, each of which is depicted briefly but in detail. One student writer begins a short story by briefly touching on a variety of images.

A grey mist descends upon Manhattan Island late Sunday

evening. At seven A.M. Monday it still shows no inclination of lifting. By then, a fine, chill drizzle accompanies it.

Millions of groggy bodies throw back the sheets, roll out of bed, peer out windows, and groan. Some dress mechanically, others with the careful precision an artist lavishes on a fine painting. Forty-five to perhaps ninety minutes later they emerge from their people-compressors. Bland faces mask stories at once varied and terribly similar—like the umbrellas they carry. The traffic snarl forces a few unfortunates to forego that important first cup of coffee.

Downtown the cabbies relish this whimsical turn of the weather. The constant tick-tick-tick of the meters and jingle-jangle of coins are crazy, jazzy melodies in their ears.

Uptown the cloistered nuns chanting matins in the chapel of Mother Cabrini Convent are, if not gleeful about the weather, at least oblivious to it. Their prayers drift heavenward with an efficacy unaffected by atmospheric variance.

A few blocks further uptown in a first floor apartment on Cabrini Boulevard, there is another who is oblivious to all the consternation. She is a woman—perhaps seventy-five—who lies curled up fetal-fashion in her down-stuffed bed. The topography of the bed is comparable to maybe the rolling hills and valleys of Kentucky. She wears a red nylon, waltz-length gown. Her silver ringlets are unloosed, nearly covering her brown-too-often-Miami-sun-tanned face.

It is not until the fifth paragraph that the writer introduces her central character. The early paragraphs establish the setting of New York—its size, and the similarity in the lives of those who live there. The writer has been selective in her details, for she wants to communicate the conformity of life in New York so that the individuality of her central character will be clearly apparent.

A description of a place can also serve indirectly to characterize a person; that is, we can partially describe individuals simply by describing their homes or their rooms. In the next excerpt a student writer describes Walter, an eccentric, likeable man who literally lives with his horses.

In the barn, horses' rumps stood in an uneven, shifting row, and varicolored tails twitched periodically from under heavy blankets. Through the many chinks in the wallboards, the snow blew in, forming little deltas of white on the stone floor. The ramshackle building was filled with munching sounds, the steam of horses' breath and smells of heavy coats, manure, and leather tack hanging on hooks along the wall. In the shed, the ponies' shaggy bodies were pressed in close, surrounding the old bathtub feed bin, stuffed with loaves of Arnold Brick Oven white, select Jewish ryes, some whole wheat and a few French and Italian loaves. Kittens of various ages ran in and out of the maze of pony legs and then disappeared behind the tub. From outside the shed came the sound of a cowbell that was tied around the goat's neck, ringing spasmodically as he moved up and down the snowy rocks outside. We hung up some of the ponies' bridles on their proper hooks—hooks that had been meticulously labeled many years ago with names of long-past ponies. From above our heads came the clomping sound of boots and of voices laughing. Walter must be upstairs we figured.

"Upstairs" was a room off the hay loft that had a four-foot high entrance way, one small window, an old refrigerator, a hot plate, a set of bunk beds, a table, and a few chairs. On the wall were pictures of Walter—one of him as a young man waving his hat, astride a huge rearing palomino in full parade trappings; another with him as a keen show rider taking his jumper over a wall-and-ditch combination fence; another as a professional trainer of thoroughbreds standing in a winner's circle; another as the founder of the "Ponies for Birthday Parties" movement, posed with a little blond girl on Frosty; and some older, indistinct pictures of him in groups of young men at some big affair in the horse world.

Though Walter himself is not directly described in this excerpt, we learn a little about his daily surroundings, his mode of life, his possessions, and his prior experiences with horses. In this description the place becomes an extension of the person who lives there. The barn and the horses are an integral part of Walter's existence.

Sometimes a place can reinforce the emotional state of the writer. The details of the room in the following selection emphasize the isolation and loneliness felt by a college student left alone in her dorm at the end of an examination period.

> I picked up the pink plastic ashtray, dumped the pear core, ugly splotch and all, into the wastebasket and plodded over to the headless twin bed nearest the window. The room was hollow and bleak with only one presence left to give it life. Sandie's exams had been over yesterday and she had left promptly to make the most of winter break. Flopping down amid the rumpled brown and orange stripes of the bedspread, I glared at the calculus book resting unperturbed on the corner desk. For two full days I had pawed over its pages while all the other cells in the dorm had gradually surrendered their prisoners for two weeks of probationary freedom. In hostile silence, I had brainwashed myself into believing I could calculate the total area, circumference, volume, and number of cans of Ajax it would take to scrub Grant's Tomb—if so requested.

From her surroundings the writer selects those details that most effectively communicate the physical disarray and emotional isolation of the room.

The practice of selecting relevant details of place to underscore a person's physical, intellectual, or emotional situation is common in fiction writing. In the following three excerpts from student short stories, descriptions of place contribute to our awareness of the central character's emotional state.

> Traces of evening dew lay on the newly green grass below Peter's feet. Dusk shadowed the playground. A lost kite hovered in the breeze above him, struggling to free itself from the clutches of the telephone wire near the slide.

It was an old kite, torn and used, and perhaps it would be better for it to hang there limply instead of venturing into the unknown. The sky was preparing to shower the earth with a gentle spring rain. And Peter was suddenly tired. Every bone in his body ached with the intensity of a pounding hammer. As if burdened by heavy weight he got up and plodded down the street toward the theater.

*   *   *

Gnawing the side of the yellow P A G pencil, Tom tensed up in his green chair at the kitchen table. He looked disgustedly at the ashtray full of cigarette butts and then rubbed his forehead trying to ease out his three-day-old headache. He ran his rough, hay-bitten fingers over his balding head. The spiciness of freshly made catsup still lingered in the kitchen. "Where to from here?" he agonized.

As he rubbed his eyes the dimly lighted, cluttered kitchen faded in and out—dirty supper dishes still on the sink, the baby's toy-scattered playpen in the corner, tomato-stained towels tossed over the backs of chairs, cans of bright red tomato juice and catsup lining Joanne's work table. Once in a while a Kerr lid popped as the last of them sealed. In the evening stillness millers buzzed around the quiet light over the sink while the water faucet dripped monotonously, irritatingly. From the bedroom the baby whimpered half-heartedly as Joanne changed his diaper and sponged the day's play off his hands, face, and feet. Outside, the youngsters shouted excitedly as they chased lightning bugs trying to capture them for their quart-jar prison.

*   *   *

Jennifer gradually sipped her iced tea. The afternoon was hot and dry, and she felt its weight like an unseen hand bearing down on her mind. Placing her glass on the arm of her patio chair, she looked up, and in a sweeping glance took in the view before her. Her brows knit as she realized how brown and ragged the lawn had become. The carefully laid sod covering the gentle sloping lawn that fell from the flagstone patio, even the hedge that marked the boundaries of their property, needed attention. Turning in her chair,

65

she was surprised by the disorder that had begun to curl around the edges of the terraced garden that flanked the right side of the patio. She sat up in her chair a little, took in the landscape deliberately for another second, and made a mental note to hire a gardener the first of next week. She didn't feel up to gardening now and wasn't sure, anyway, just how to approach these ragged blooms. Jason had never allowed anyone but himself to care for the yard.

In the first selection the writer focuses on a playground. Through a description of the surroundings, we learn a good deal about Peter's state of mind. The shadows of dusk that envelop the playground reflect his feelings of futility and defeat. The torn kite hovering above suggests his uncertainty and lack of fulfillment. The oncoming spring rain seems to wash away his defenses, leaving him suddenly weary. The cause of Peter's condition is unknown, but his dismay is apparent. In the second selection the writer introduces a tense, middle-aged farmer. He has had a headache for three days; he has been smoking regularly; and he has a serious decision to make. To reinforce the disarray of the farmer's mind and feelings, the writer focuses on the physical disarray of his surroundings—dirty dishes, whimpering child, dripping faucet, and the especially suggestive red-stained towels. The last selection also uses place to underscore Jennifer's state of mind. She feels a weight bearing down on her; her brows are knit; and she is mildly perplexed. Appropriately, her surroundings are in need of care: the lawn is brown; the flowers are ragged; the garden is becoming disordered. Later in the story we learn that Jennifer's life needs attention, just as the garden and lawn need attention.

Descriptions of place need not always be serious or restricted to realistic prose. You might enjoy experimenting with a variety of techniques and styles. One student used verse to communicate his view of Woodstock.

W hat a place to be
O n some cat's beautiful farm
O ut in the boondocks of New York

D riving is a trip
S leeping in
T ents
O n the ground
C hicks all over the place
K issing everyone in sight

M usic is fantastic even
U nder the drenching rain
S inging and running nude
I n a sea of mud with any foxy
C hick in sight

A ll the really big rock stars are here
N O PIGS
D on't bogart that joint

A ll day and night the music plays
R eaching all the way back to the one
T housandth row of people

F ive hundred thousand freaks
A nd heavies
I n one place
R ocking out and having a good and peaceful time.

Though the meter is forced at times and the lines are clearly manipulated to fit the requirements of the vertical spelling, the verse nevertheless is entertaining. The writer is able to communicate the free, festive atmosphere at Woodstock.

Another alternative is to express an exaggerated, fantasized or comic view of a place. One student writer has imaginatively recalled her first piano lesson. Told in quasi-fairy tale style, the following excerpt emphasizes the child's metaphoric interpretation of both the piano teacher and her house.

Tall oaks urgently fanned the eaves of the two-story white frame house atop Park Street Hill. Glints of summer sunlight darted speckled patterns upon the newly mowed lawn. Peggy paused at the picket gate, twirling a blonde pigtail through the chubby fingers of her right hand. In the left she clutched tightly the dollar bill Mother had given her for her first piano lesson. The little black spaniel at her heels brushed encouragingly against her legs. Peggy knelt down, put her tiny arms about his neck, and nestled a suntanned cheek in the silky coat. "I have to go in now, Jinx. You wait here for me; I won't be long."

The old house blinked a curtained eyelid and seemed to hiccup as Peggy stood up. The front door sprung open and burped forth a mountain of grey and purple paisley, complete with capped peak of plaited snow hair. The great grey figure pasted pointed, quavering words on the darting sunspots "Are you Peggy Rogers? You're late! Don't dawdle, you have just a half hour, and you're wasting it, dearie. Hurry on now; and leave your doggy home next time. Animals make my allergy flare up." Then heaving her bulk abruptly about, the old house gulped, and she was gone.

Peggy bent to give Jinx's head a final pet and with a deep sigh, clenched teeth, and squared shoulders, opened the gate and marched one patent-leathered foot after the other firmly up the cement tongue, opened the door, and let the old house lick her up too. The door smacked shut behind her as she viewed a long rose hall with three white doors on either side, all shut. The seventh door at the end of the hall was open. Peggy's feet made no noise on the maroon carpet as she crossed the hall and peered in. Inside was a world of brown: tweed-brown carpet, coffee-brown leather recliner in a far corner, tobacco-brown overstuffed chair in another, walnut-brown end tables, sandlewood-brown walls, russet-brown curtains, and from the ceiling a hanging chandelier of hobnailed, amber-brown globes. The paisley mountain perched itself precariously on the edge of a crushed peanut-brown, velvet Queen Anne chair next to the pecan-colored upright spinet. Peggy wished she had worn brown; somehow her lemon-colored polka dotted pinafore seemed awfully bright in the shade of so much woodhue.

You may, of course, write about place in a more sustained and thorough way than the previous examples have suggested. Some places have significant meaning for us, and thus require more detailed treatment in writing. In "On the Making of Cities" (page 20), which we discussed earlier, the writer relates her childhood experiences in a specific location. She focuses on place to unify her autobiographical essay and describes how important places from the past have changed, thereby changing her life. Often the places that hold most meaning for us are those associated with our pasts. For each of us there are a few places—a house, a neighborhood, a summer cottage, a clubhouse—that evoke strong responses from us. Writing about these places requires your careful attention, for it is important that you avoid lapsing into sentimental generalizations about the mystery of your grandmother's attic or the seclusion of your favorite tree house. To fully express the meaning a place holds for you, it is necessary to communicate the details of that place as completely and as concretely as you can.

In "A Ceaseless Need" the student writer describes the ocean as a place that has special significance in her life. She recalls days of youthful pleasure when she thoroughly enjoyed the sea. She goes on to explain her rejection of the sea, and finally she expresses her desire to return to it once more. Notice that the narrator sometimes uses concrete language; but when she neglects to select her language precisely, the paper loses its intensity.

A CEASELESS NEED

Has it really been so long since I've seen the sea? It really couldn't be, since my mind and body so vividly recall it with an acute, poignant longing. I'm terribly homesick for its pungent smell and the sound of its breakers crashing on the rock jetties, protruding like gnarled fingers from the sandy shore. I can still see it sliding onto the clean, white beach, gradually coming closer and closer to me as I sit alone on the shore with the screeching gulls for company. I remember how it looks on a quiet, moonlit night—serene and peaceful—and how on the next day it can change, lashing out in gray-green anger as a storm rages through it. How I love the way it feels! It was always so icy cold as I took my first plunge of the season. What a marvelous sensation it was to ride in on those waves on a rubber raft, frequently being tossed, twisted, and finally dumped onto the shore—a sandy, salty heap in a multicolored swimsuit. Then I'd lie on my back in the warm sand, rapidly becoming so scorched by the sun's penetrating rays that I had to go back for more of the sea's delicious punishment. Four years may seem a short time for some, but for me it has been too long a time to be separated from the sea.

My love affair with the sea has been a strong one for many years. I was merely a child of six when I first ran along the beach and viewed its deep green breakers iced with frothy white. That was the start of our love affair. How those booming waves and screaming gulls communicated with me! I could turn to the sea as to an understanding friend whenever I was afraid or lonely, without fear of rebuke. I also went to the sea when I was filled with childish delight, running along the beach for the sheer joy of being there and creating magnificent architectural designs in the sand.

As I grew older, I learned the diverse moods of the sea and felt they often joined with mine as I experienced many-faceted adolescence. Although the sea was moody and temperamental, it remained a constant in my life— a stable factor in a continuously changing world. No matter what its mood, the sea was always there for me with its breakers crashing on the shore, moving in and out with the tide.

But one day, as is inevitable in any love affair, I suppose, the sea turned evil and deceived me. I had realized all along that this might happen, had actually feared it but had always pushed it aside in my mind. My wonderful, friendly love turned into a vicious killer and took away someone who was very important and close to me. The sea grabbed his strong, tan body as if it were a child's toy doll, pulling him under with the strong, unpredictable current. He could not find the strength to fight the sea and was lost. The sea relinquished his body, throwing it ashore in a nearly unidentifiable bloated condition.

I cursed the sea and cried out in disbelief. Why had the sea done this to a strong young boy? Why had the sea done this to me? Why was I so deceived? Hadn't I always been a faithful friend? The only response was the waves moving onto the shore. The sea did not answer my cries and certainly could not console me, since it had caused my misery.

I couldn't stand being near the sea any longer. I hated it and what it had done to me—the pain and discomfort it had caused. In an attempt to seek revenge and to forget, I turned my back on the sea and came out here.

I thought for awhile that I was contented. I had conquered the sea and my need for it. But as the months went by, much of my pain was softened by time. I learned to care for other strong young boys, while the murdered one became a hazy memory, always tinged with pleasure and pain. In my dreams old visions began reappearing with ever increasing frequency. I found that my old longings for the presence of the sea had been completely rekindled. I now feel a strong, almost overpowering compulsion to be near it again.

When friends hear me talk of the sea, they assure me that I should be able to find a fulfillment for my longings out here. Lake Michigan is not far, they remind me. I laugh when they tell me this. I know they are truly sincere and well-meaning, but they don't understand the power that the sea has over me. I've known it for so long as a friend, confidant, and love that Lake Michigan would stand as a very poor second to my sea.

That's why I must go back again. I have been away long enough. The sea has a strong hold over me that I can no longer deny. Although it has deceived me, I must realize that it has also conquered me. With less trust than before, but with strong love and respect, I am going back to the sea.

The sea in this selection is more than an isolated memory for the narrator. It is a place that holds a mixture of emotional associations and meanings; a place that is intricately woven into the texture of her childhood and adolescence. She can partially measure her growth through her changing perceptions of and responses to the sea.

What is most lacking in the paper is the consistent use of details. Too often the writer relies on glib or tired phrases ("marvelous sensation," "many-faceted adolescence," "my wonderful friendly lover"). At times, however, her language is precise and graphic. She describes the sea "lashing out in gray-green anger" and the rock jetties "protruding like gnarled fingers from the sandy shore." The death of the friend is treated obliquely. Once again the language is not carefully selected. The boy is inadequately described as "someone who was very important and close to me." Though it is clear that the writer is emotionally torn by the incident, the vague language prevents the reader from experiencing the loss. Only the "nearly unidentifiable bloated condition" of the boy's body carries an impact. Despite the frequent use of imprecise language, however, "A Ceaseless Need" does illustrate how a place can contribute continuing meaning to our lives.

In the next selection the narrator describes her sister's bedroom in a manner that also describes both the younger girl and the relationship between the sisters.

JO'S ROOM

In the hall I hesitated. I'd been away from home for a long time and had almost forgotten those beige-fleshy tinted walls. Now light filtered through cheese cloth curtains at the top of the stairs, scattering a handful of brilliant freckles across the walls and me. I stood for a moment trying to see if I could feel sunshine warmth in spots, but of course I couldn't. I turned to the door and reached out for the brass knob, feeling vibrations of a stretching spring as the latch drew back inside the wooden frame. My sister always did keep her door shut, even when we were little girls. Not just pushed closed as an afterthought when she hurried away, but firmly, deliberately pulled until it latched. I went into her room on invitation mostly or sneaked in to borrow perfume when I could hear her racking through Chopin or gliding with Brahms across the piano keys downstairs.

Today I was looking for her tweezers and although I knew she had rushed off to the sailing regatta on campus, I still had found myself balancing on the edge of the fourth step to keep it from squeaking when I crept up the stairs. Even now as I opened the door and looked into the room, I felt like a rookie second-story man, and that was silly because we'd outgrown that childish sense of possession long ago. Jo would have brought me the tweezers herself if I had asked while she was home.

Without stepping in I looked around the room. Funny how I had memorized it. Usually I don't think much about details, but here was a fantasy display of small, strange objects carefully selected from the world of bottom drawers, dime store windows, occupant mail, ceramics class, and the back yard. My eyes traced the edges of the room as a woman would run her finger over a coffee table to check for dust. To the right of the door the tall, honey-mellowed chest of drawers held its usual favorites: in the back, a Japanese transistor radio with one plastic corner chipped off and replaced with Elmer's glue, and ten or fifteen rings in a lumpy, yellow china bowl in front of the dials on the radio. A gray flannel mouse with no eyes and a red heart sewn to the end of his ribbon tail stared at the door. Centered and behind the mouse, a man-sized box of Kleenex, done appropriately in red handkerchief print, offered its tousled square of white to anyone. And monopolizing the front, three figurines of parade horses marched head to tail, bravely defying anyone to tread heavily and rock them off. These and a few smaller items all perched on Gramma's ivory dresser scarf with the prim lavender and gold tatted edge.

Leaning in through the doorway with my head, I saw her desk—actually a small drop-leaf table dully blue in the corner. It held shapes like tilted picture frames, toothpaste tubes rolled tight, one bookend *sans* books, and a stack of something, probably papers. I couldn't really see for certain because, although the window was just beyond the desk on the other wall, its yellowed shade had been pulled early this morning. The room glowed like a toy made from a shoe box with a cotton batting floor and a scene cut from an old Sears catalogue, the whole thing being covered with golden tissue paper. The light was evenly dispersed and translucent but made everything seem dull with its lack of shadows. To the left of the window was Jo's bed, a canopy with pink-skirted ballerinas dancing across the spread and roof. Lord, hadn't she gotten rid of that by now after a whole year in college? My eyes traced the shapes—against the opposite wall beneath the second window, the rocking chair and wooden bench held assorted bottles and jars. How anyone could manage to put eye liner on straight while rocking is beyond me. Then I smiled at myself. Of course Jo didn't wear eye make-up, never had. Well, I had to get the tweezers. I ventured in quietly, leaving the door open behind me. I bent down closer to identify the bottles—Genuine Rosewater and Glycerin, Water Lily Pore Cleanser, Maja perfume, and a capless bottle of sand from Lake Michigan. And there right in front of the sand was a newspaper clipping mounted on red flannel and cardboard and framed with a ridge of gold glitter stuck on with Elmer's glue. I picked it up gingerly, careful not to disturb any loose sparkles and lifted it up to my eyes, although I didn't have to read the article. I had a copy myself for my scrapbook. "Local graduates from Michigan State University include Mary Atkins, daughter of Mr. and Mrs. Henry Atkins of Allendale. . . . " The sequined specks began to leap and pirouette on their red carpet as my hand began to shake. I had been in her room all the time.

Though the younger sister never actually appears in this brief sketch, we learn a great deal about her. Jo's room reveals her habits, interests, and experiences. She has accumulated an assortment of possessions that are scattered throughout the room in no apparent order. She is not a neat housekeeper but appears to enjoy living in comfortable disarray among objects that are "old friends."

She also enjoys her privacy, for she deliberately latches her door when she leaves the room. Aware of this custom, the narrator is reluctant to invade the privacy of the room. She apprehensively views it as a place where she does not rightfully belong. When she discovers her graduation picture carefully decorated and displayed on Jo's bench, she then realizes that she has always been a valued part of Jo's private world.

The narrator's vivid description of the room and her frank hesitation to enter it uninvited enable the reader to share the brief episode with the older sister. She does not dismiss the condition of the room by simply describing it as being cluttered with outgrown childhood possessions or odds and ends of souvenirs and junk. Instead she concretely relates the details of what she sees. By allowing us to join her on the abbreviated tour of the premises, she gives us a glimpse into the lives of both girls.

"Jo's Room" treats place in a relatively static manner. In the next paper the writer recreates her childhood activities and experiences in an apple orchard. She revives her memories so precisely that the reader is able to experience the place with her.

APPLE ORCHARD

I could never understand why people wanted their property all neat and mowed. A perfectly trimmed lawn with its flowered borders and pruned trees was about as exciting as taking a bath and putting on a dress.

Such lawns drove my best friend and myself to the apple orchard. Every weed that lived there held a discovery for us. Some weeds contained thousands of fluffy white puffs with seeds attached to the end. We'd break open the pods they were in and blow the puffs out of our hands. Queen Anne's lace and creamy-filled milkweed, dandelions and tumbleweeds, built a jungle of adventure. Camouflaged thistle and the well-known burr soon won our respect. Their magnetic attraction to our hair and clothing brought forth the wrath of our mothers. "Tomboy," they'd call us. "Why don't you play dolls and have tea parties like other girls?"

The apple trees were perfect for climbing. Their

neglected branches proved efficient ladders to homemade tree houses balanced on crooked limbs. In the summer when the leaves were thick, no one could see us, not even the crummy Ridenour kids. Not only were these apple trees perfect for clubhouses, but they provided an extra bonus—apples. These apples weren't at all like the ones you got at the store; that made them even better. These apples started out like hard, little green grapes, grew and grew, turned red, and then fell to the ground. They were small and strangely shaped, and when you bit into one, your mouth coated with a dry, tongue-curling juice. After eating one or two it felt like someone had scraped your teeth with a fingernail file.

The apple trees were great, but the best thing was the chicken coop. It was an old, deserted shack with many dried remains, compliments of the chickens. To us this was a royal stable. This small five-by-five coop contained fifty horses. Stalls were partitioned with twine. The heavy-work horses were in the far right corner, carriage and saddle horses in the far left, ponies close right, and racers and jumpers in the near left. We gathered tall, thin weeds for hay, sawdust for oats, and grass for bedding. We rode miles across country on these horses. The missions we fulfilled on horseback would fill a book.

Dark came quickly in the apple orchard. Our mothers called us in for supper long before our day was done.

This selection is filled with concrete details. The narrator includes sense impressions (similar to those we discussed in Chapter 3) to convey her experience in the orchard. She remembers the "fluffy white puffs" that the girls blew from their hands and the tart red apples that coated their teeth. Even more than the sensation and physical reality of the orchard is included in the description; the narrator also relates her childhood adventures—the allure the orchard held for the two young "tomboys." The orchard offered an escape from the ladylike decorum of a "trimmed lawn" and "tea parties." Their behavior in the orchard was imaginative and adventurous: they explored a weed-filled "jungle," climbed apple trees, managed a "royal stable," and fulfilled many "missions."

Though the selection is brief and ends rather abruptly, the narrator has reconstructed her experiences in the orchard to concretely convey the meaning it had for her.

The examples included in this chapter suggest only a few ways to write about place; there are many other possibilities. You might write about a place you have imagined but have never actually visited; you could choose to describe a series of places that have influenced your life; or you might even express your need to have a special place of your own. Whatever your specific topic, you will want to select your language carefully and design your paper so that it clearly conveys your meaning. A place can be a momentary, picturesque, deserted scene or a complex blend of rooms, people, events, and human emotion. If you recognize that a place can be both a physical location and a situation, your writing will be richer and more perceptive.

APPROPRIATE WRITING MODES

You may employ a variety of techniques and voices to write about place.

Possible forms: Lists, fragments, sketches, or more complete narrative prose—even essays—are acceptable modes for describing or capturing place.

Possible points of view: You can describe a place from the first, second, or third person, and you can experiment with the time sequence—that is, describe the place as observed now or as it is remembered.

Possible methods of focus: You might experiment with writing that ranges from subjective response to a place to more objective emphasis on the place itself.

SPECIFIC WRITING POSSIBILITIES

Describe specific people or things seen or heard in a particular place at a particular time (for example, campus cafeteria, a football game, library, drugstore, cocktail party, and so on).

Explain or respond to what is happening at a specific place and location, in such a way that the details create a specific impression.

Describe your reaction to a place that has an intense emotional effect on you.

Write a brief, indirect character sketch of yourself by focusing on a place you like or dislike.

Describe a place from more than one perspective (for example, a carnival, from the point of view of a child, of a huckster, of a maiden aunt, of a county sheriff, and so on).

Describe a house, an office, or a room, so that you are indirectly describing the person who lives there.

Describe how your responses to a place have changed as you have grown older.

Describe a place that was important to you or influenced you as a child.

Describe a place that no longer has the strong effect on you it once had. You might choose a tavern that was mysterious or alluring to you as a child, the neighborhood ghost house, a hospital, a pleasant country meadow, an attic, or even a foreign country. Try to include both your earlier and your present responses or experiences.

Dramatize an experience that changed your opinion of the place where it happened (for example, an experience at a ski lodge, in a dormitory, at a dance, at a vacation cottage, in a foreign country, and so on).

Explain the way you associate a particular place with an important person or event in your life.

relating to others

The persons, places, and things of our lives of course have a solid physical existence of their own, which anybody in encounter with them would deny at peril of stubbing his toe or bruising his ego. But, again, the realities we live with are those that we create in the linguistic imagination and carry about with us in mind and memory. We turn a person into a friend, a place into a room for reverie, a thing into a keepsake charged with strong feelings. And we write all of these into the running narratives of our ceaselessly flowing, continuously altering lives.

JAMES MILLER
Word, Self, Reality

I discover who I am through exploration of all the relationships of my experience, for I am created only in the experiences of those relationships.

MARTIN BUBER
I and Thou

Just as your encounters with yourself and with place help form your identity and your perception of the world, so can your relationships with other people—parents, grandparents, sisters, brothers, friends, teachers, rivals—strongly influence your growth and development. By examining and writing about these relationships you can begin to learn how they have shaped your life and how they have contributed to your perceptions of yourself and of others.

Our longest and most intense relationships probably have the greatest influence on our lives. We increase our understanding of ourselves and others when we characterize those people we have known for long periods of time and analyze our relations with them. These relationships also serve as a measure of our growth— our development. As we grow and change, the relationships will change, and we can begin to evaluate and define their meaning. Since it is often difficult for us to look carefully at our complex relationships with others, writing about close relationships requires our thoughtful and honest consideration.

Not all our associations with others are lasting or intense, however; many are limited, superficial, or impersonal. But writing about these encounters also requires careful attention, and even though the association may be casual or impersonal, the writing cannot be careless. We must select words that communicate as precisely as possible what we want to say about that casual relationship. Sometimes we simply observe or describe people without knowing them or dealing with them, but even in this case we should observe carefully. If we are going to write about others or about limited relationships in any but an external way, we must engage in some interaction or relationship—actual or imagined— with that person. We must to some extent imaginatively perceive the other's experience. What do you suppose the street beggar feels? How does the cab driver view the world? What kind of family life does the salesclerk have? What dreams or goals does your mailman have? What might a construction worker write in a journal? All these questions require us to imaginatively exchange places with another person.

Writing about others draws you even further out from your initial encounters with self. In this chapter I am encouraging you to reach out beyond your own life to the lives and realities of others. When you write about others, you will soon learn that each of us leads a many-faceted life. We function, for instance, as men or women, as sons or daughters, as siblings or only children. Even a young person functions in several roles—as a student, a son, a Boy Scout, a paperboy, a dog owner, and so on. As he grows older, these roles become even more diverse. Your responses to other people are usually based on your limited experience with them as they function in only one or two of these roles. You know Sally as a classmate or roommate, not as a daughter; you know Mr. Miller as Jack's father, not as an employer; you know the lady next door as a dog hater, not as the wife of a handicapped husband. From your limited experiences with a friend or acquaintance you create your image of him or her.

When you write about other people, you may discover that you view them in only one or two of these roles. Undoubtedly you will also discover the limits of your own perceptions about them. You may not know, for example, what their political opinions are. You may not understand how they feel about their family or friends. You may not be able to imagine what their inner flow of language is like.

Paradoxically, the very act of reaching out toward others helps you to become more aware of yourself. In writing about other people you learn not only about their reality but also about your responses, your modes of perceiving, and the limits of your perceptions. You will learn a good deal about yourself, for as Buber says we are indeed composed of all the relationships we experience.

Before you begin writing, you might consider how you look at others and what you actually see. How do you respond when you first meet people? What influences your initial responses? Perhaps you first notice physical characteristics—the age, sex, color and length of hair, the physique or figure, height, facial expression, frequency and sincerity of smiles, eye color, voice quality and pitch. Often, details such as calloused hands, dirt under fingernails, slouched posture, rasping cough, or appearance of clothes tell you about a person's health, attitude, occupation, emotional state, or self-image. You also may notice movements and gestures. How does the girl walk? Does the salesman punctuate his sentences by jabbing his finger at you? Does the boy avoid meeting your glance? Does the young reporter anxiously nibble at the eraser of her pencil? You notice all these things, and they influence your responses even before you exchange any words with a person. How often, in fact, do you quickly judge and dismiss people you have just met? What contributes to your hasty conclusions? By carefully observing others, you may become more conscious of how another person's physical features or behavior affect you. You might also begin to distinguish the difference between describing what you see and interpreting what you see.

To write effectively about others, you must carefully examine the persons and your responses to them. You also must choose words that concretely communicate those details and responses. You will want to use more than mere abstract labels (such as loving, hateful, generous, meticulous, or irresponsible) to describe others. To label a man as dishonest, for example, is not nearly so effective as demonstrating his dishonesty with examples, actions, or dialogue. Telling us your grandmother is kind and generous may not be as convincing as providing a sketch that illustrates those qualities by example. Readers are usually more convinced when they are allowed some opportunity to observe the person themselves.

To help you find appropriate details for your writing, you might examine the process by which you have arrived and continue to arrive at conclusions about other people. When you write, you are, in a sense, reliving that process on paper, being highly selective in the details you include. You are asked to be keenly observant of yourself, of the other person, and of the interaction—passive or active—between the two of you. When you see an old lady waiting for a bus, what do you notice about her, and how do you react to what you notice? What do you notice about the young boy who delivers your newspaper, or about the cashier at the bank? What conclusions do you draw from what you see? Do you tend to categorize people? Do some people strike you as conservative, stingy, or rigid, while others appear generous, independent, or flexible? What details lead you to respond in this way? Do you make up stories about strangers you see? What physical characteristics influence your imaginary response? Considering these questions may lead you to write a more detailed characterization.

Notice the physical details in the following description. The writer begins by noting the woman's fatigue. The description then goes on to include specific details that allow us to observe the woman's appearance.

> Fatigued, as though every muscle in her body begs for rest after the day's work, a young woman, perhaps in her early thirties, stands propped against the wooden part of her doorway, looking out at something that I cannot see. Her pink and white checked blouse, trimmed with ruffles and lace (yet revealing a careless double crease pressed into the right shoulder) clashes violently with the red and white striped skirt which bulges awkwardly over the eight-month-old child that lies sleeping inside her. Dragged forward by this extra weight, her back arches drastically, causing only her shoulders and one elbow to support her stance against the wall. Smooth and straight, lacking the normal curves, her arms hang tensed at her sides, her right hand clenching tightly at her skirt.

This description grew from a class discussion about how we perceive others. The specific assignment was rather complex. The students were asked to select a stranger and then write down their reactions to and conclusions about the person. Next they chose some general terms (nervous, energetic, handsome, discouraged, and so on) to describe the subject. This was followed by a close examination of the person to determine, if possible, what physical characteristics or movements contributed to the writer's initial reaction. Finally, they composed a description that included both the physical details and some of their personal reactions so that the reader would agree with the assessment.

The next characterization concentrates almost wholly on the physical features and gestures of a stranger.

> A harsh light diffused through a ceiling fixture in the sterile waiting room at Olin Health Center. The dark rays fell on the woman's flimsy, threadbare hat, but not on the ancient Negro face beneath it. Buried in this dark shadow was a stained faced, shriveled by a network of deeply carved wrinkles. Over the coarsened complexion, beads of perspiration sluggishly filled each crevice. From

behind swollen lids dull, yellowed eyes studied a 1964 June issue of *Reader's Digest,* deeply buried in the folds of her outdated skirt. An arthritic finger uncontrollably shook while pointing at the small print, although it remained perched over the same word. Taut flesh stretched over the knuckles of the other hand, which tightly grasped the ragged damp remains of a piece of Kleenex used in intervals to sweep across her moistened forehead. The strange odor of Dixie Peach Hair Dressing intermingling with the fresh scent of a menthol cough drop lingered in the air above her. Her only movement consisted of occasionally lifting her eyes and focusing on the wall clock, with hands pointed accusingly at the late hours of afternoon. When the loudspeaker blurted a name, a flash of recognition darted across her expressionless face. Then so slowly, as if carrying the weight of the world, the woman hoisted her full body and wearily dragged herself down the long corridor.

Notice how carefully the writer chooses words that contribute to the tone and setting of the paper. Words such as *sterile, stark, ancient, strained, shriveled, coarsened, sluggishly, taut, ragged* all depict the bleakness that pervades the entire description.

Describing physical characteristics is, of course, only one way of writing about others. We can also record what they say. Our conversations with others obviously contribute to our perceptions of them. We are influenced by people's voices, for instance—their pitch, quality, intensity, speed, and so on. And, naturally, we are influenced by their opinions, problems, experiences, interests, and actions. We also learn about a person from others; for instance, we learn about political candidates by listening to what they tell us, but we also learn by listening to what others say about them. We can emphasize speech in a characterization. It is possible, for instance, to describe people simply by recording a conversation in which they participate.

The following exchange between two girls was written by a freshman writer.

"Are you sure you want this done? I don't want to be held responsible for your ears the rest of my life!"

"Yea, go ahead. I'm ready."

"Okay, but don't change your mind after I'm started, unless you only want one ear pierced. I think that would be nice."

"No thanks, I'll take two."

"Okay, where's the ice? I brought you the alcohol and the earrings. I even cleaned the paint off my hands for ya."

"Oh, those are the earrings you made! Thanks a lot, they're the ones I wanted."

"Yea well, hold this against your ear. No, I'll hang onto it. Guess what? I sold a ring the other day. I don't know how anyone can live off their artwork. I'll probably live on peanut butter the rest of my life."

"Hey, this is beginning to hurt."

"No, it's not, it's just freezing. Don't be a baby now. Okay, I think you're ready. Got the needle through."

"What are you doing?"

"I can't get the wire through. Don't worry, I just can't find the hole in back. Oh, there it goes."

"Is my ear bleeding?"

"Yea man, it's green! oooh look at it run over your shoulder and down your back! Hey, while you're waiting for the other ear, I can do your nose as a bonus!"

The conversation is a simple one; yet we do learn about the two speakers, particularly the girl who is performing the "operation." She is an artist who works with paint and makes jewelry too—some of which she has sold. She is willing to give her friend a pair of earrings, and she has a sense of humor. All this is communicated indirectly to the reader. Though there is almost nothing said about the setting, or the gestures, movements, or vocal inflections of the participants, the conversation does characterize the two girls.

The next conversation also omits direct references to the setting and to the tone of voice of the speakers. Yet once again we do learn about the speakers and their relationship to one another.

CHARACTER SKETCH

A conversation on the telephone between boy and girl

Phone rings and someone answers.
"Hello, is Shelley there?"
"Yes, just a minute."
"Hello."
"Hi, how are you Shelley."
"What do you want?"
"I just wanted to talk."
"Oh, really. What about?"
"Nothing in particular. Boy, wasn't it nice weather out today?"
"I thought it was kind of dull and gloomy."
"But the sun was shining and it was really beautiful."
"Maybe on your side of town it was, but not on mine!"
"But we live right next to each other."
"I know but we are different."
"Well, how have you been lately?"
"Not too good."
"How come?"
"People keep bothering me."
"Am I bothering you by calling you up?"
"Well . . ."
"Well what?"
"I just can't stand talking to people any more."
"What you really mean is that you can not stand me?"
A pause for a few minutes. Then she finally says:
"Well, I have to go, see you later."
"Bye."
"Goodbye."

The boy in this sketch is obviously interested in Shelley, but the girl's abrupt answers and flippant manner indicate her lack of interest in both the boy and their relationship. Yet she isn't quite candid enough to explain her feelings or lack of them. When the boy finally asks her to state her feelings directly, she evades the issue by retreating.

We often discover when we try to describe people, even those we love or think we know well, that we don't know a great deal about them. By writing a paper from other people's perspectives, you may better understand them and learn how to characterize them more fully. You will be trying to reproduce their views of the world, their thoughts, and their opinions in a convincing manner. Can you, for instance, write a page that might appear in your sister's or mother's journal? Can you reproduce your grandfather's thoughts—a kind of stream of consciousness writing from his point of view? Here is how one student tried to capture the thoughts of a lonely old woman.

Seems like I've been in bed now for such a long time.
There's just nothing else to do. You get so lonely here.
No one to talk to, that's why as soon as I wake up I always
turn the radio on. There's got to be some noise; otherwise
I would be like the lady upstairs—crazy. I used to have
a TV and I'd watch that all of the time. That was before John
died. I wish he were still here. At least you knew someone
else was in the place with you and you didn't get so lonely.
He wasn't much company the last years 'cause he layed
in bed and coughed all of the time. They said it was because
of all of the sores he had on him. Said they got in his throat
and choked him to death. Seems to me they could have
done something if they had tried. They got cures for everything else. I got some sores, funny ones, but they're not the
same. Anyway I can't watch the TV anymore because they
stole it. Just came in and took it. Said I hadn't made the
payments on it. It left that wall over there kind of empty
looking.

There used to be the kids, but they're all gone. Jim
moved to Denver. He's a big lawyer there, pretty important
I guess. Wish he would write once in a while. Mary got
married to a preacher; took her to Canada. I haven't seen her
in six or seven years. She didn't even come home when
John died. Said something about not being able to. Always
wondered what she saw in that preacher.

Guess I don't eat much anymore. That's probably why
I don't feel so good a lot of the time. Maybe that's why
I cough a lot. It's just no good cooking for yourself. I used to

really like cooking for the four of us. Everyone around the table joking and laughing, telling all about school. I haven't done the dishes lately. I just can't get around like I used to.

I used to have a special day. I used to get all dressed up and wait for the mailman to come and bring my check and then I'd call the cab to take me shopping. I used to go shopping at the biggest store I have ever seen. The people there were so nice to me, they even knew my name.

"Yes, Mrs. Wescott, I'll get it for you."

"Yes, Mrs. Wescott, I'll see if we have it in the back."

"No, Mrs. Wescott, we didn't get any in today."

I used to even ask for things I knew they didn't have just to see them run for me. I liked to be able to tell them to do something and they would do it for me. That was before the one long-haired boy told me not to bother him anymore and told me to go shop somewhere else. I don't care to go there anymore. Come to think of it, I haven't been out of here since.

I've been coughing a lot lately. It's awfully lonely here.

The writer has attempted to tap the inner language of the old woman in a way that characterizes her past and present life. We learn that in the past she was financially independent. She once enjoyed a pleasant family life, though now her grown children neglect her. Her present life is characterized by loneliness, financial need, and poor health.

Description of physical details, dialogue, and interior monologue are only three techniques for writing about others. Character sketches may also describe behavior, actions, or settings. Most characterizations, in fact, combine all of these—physical features, dialogue, actions, and setting. And all of them can be communicated through a variety of modes of writing. You might begin, for instance, by collecting some isolated phrases about a character and shaping them into a kind of poetic format something like the following:

gray balding hair and a clean shaven face
dressed in his favorite pants and flannel shirt
he tries to keep a slow and steady pace

his ever brilliant smile reveals itself as he watches children
    playing outside
being hard of hearing he strains to catch their words
wishing that in him they might confide
when standing straight he's six foot three inches tall
with arm muscles slightly bulging he reaches for balance
    to the walls
he's becoming thinner in his later years
his once deep brown eyes seem to hold less color now
to those who hold him dear
he's not an uncommon aging man
he's just living out his years.

Another student writer cast her character sketch in the form of a
letter that includes references to the subject's physical appearance,
dialogue, and actions.

Dear Jim Beach:

Where are you? Probably about July I'll see you strolling
down the waterfront on Sandy Island. Such an appropriate
name—Beach; I've never seen you anywhere but on the
beach. And always in the same jeans and green undershirt
that barely covers your six feet of bones, and your boating
shoes that never are tied. I hope you still have some hair
left—other than those long strands that look as though they'd
been pasted indiscriminately on your head. I'm sorry . . .
It's just that you look like you might fade away.

   Remember that summer when you used to walk down the
beach every night after dinner to see Mr. Miller, the fifty-
year-old architect? He thought he was pretty groovy, rapping
with a hippie. Could he ever tell you anything?

   I remember the first time I met you we were all at Miller's
cottage watching the first moon landing. You were sitting
in a corner watching—being your usual nonverbal self.
Something was wrong with the television, and everytime
the set would black out, you'd throw a penny at it, and the
picture would miraculously return.

   I was just sitting here wondering if you're living alone

in a tepee in Arizona like you said. Were you serious when you said you didn't need anyone—anyone? I do know, though, for a fact, that you're not in Texas. "Nothing good has ever happened to me in Texas . . . The last time I was hitchhiking through Texas, two girls picked me up and raped me. They took me out in a field, at gunpoint made me take off all my clothes, and then looked me over like a side of beef."

Where are you, Jim? Where do you go in the winter when you can't just float along the beach and when you can't sleep on any dock where you might happen to fall. I just thought I'd write and ask—in case I happen to miss your phenomenal appearing and disappearing act this summer.

Oh—if you ever again get the chance to play with B. B. King, tell him I said Hi.

The letter form allows the writer to talk directly to her friend. In this way we not only learn about Jim, we also learn how she relates to him. Her choice of words and the tone of the letter express her warm but casual relationship with him.

Many of these early examples are descriptions of strangers or casual friends. You may, in fact, find it easier to begin writing physical descriptions of strangers, since with them you are better able to examine and separate your perceptions. You may also find it easier to separate your perceptions from your reactions. When you try to describe someone you know well, the challenge is greater, for your emotional reactions are so closely tied with the physical characteristics that you are more likely to rely on generalization than on detail. Stop for a moment and list the adjectives that come to mind when you think of your mother, father, grandmother, sister, wife, child, or boyfriend. Then try to list four or five specific details, actions, or incidents that illustrate those characteristics. From this material you then might begin to write a sketch that will encourage your reader to respond as you do. It may help to start once again with basic physical features or gestures or perhaps some isolated images that come to mind when you think of the person. This will be especially helpful when you write about someone you knew as a child. In this brief sketch the writer gathers together some details he remembers about his grandfather:

He was tall, thickly bearded, always ho, ho, ho-ing, and
he wore suspenders under his frayed pinstripe suit.
He sported, along with his beard, a great handlebar
moustache. His hands were like old hardened pieces of
tanned leather. This was Grandpa.
There stuck from his smiling mouth of ivory teeth a pipe.
He was constantly smoking. When he was happy he'd sit
back and chuckle contentedly, but when he disagreed with
something he smoked vehemently. To me, who sat on his lap,
it seemed like great billowing clouds of smoke rose upward
from his pipe.
When he came over, he brought taffy on sticks or huge
suckers. You could tell when he was sneaking up on you.
Either you could feel those great smiling eyes on you or smell
the sweetness of his pipe. That's Grandpa.

Though the student's thoughts are presented in a random manner
with no meaningful links between them, the writing experience
does stimulate the writer's memory and encourage him to recreate
the incidents in some detail.

As a follow-up exercise, try to organize a collection of
images in a more meaningful sequence. You could order your
memories of a person so that they trace the development either of
that person or, on the other hand, of yourself. In the following
sketch the writer not only describes her father; she is also recording her changing perceptions of him. Notice, too, how the writer
characterizes her father with dialogue, physical description, and
specific behavior.

PIECES OF A PORTRAIT
FOUND WHILE TRAVELING THROUGH CHILDHOOD

"Kenneth, the kids are coming in to have you wash their
hands. Supper's almost ready."
"All right. Come on. Ladies first."
I stood no taller than the washbowl and held my hands
up expectantly. He dipped them in the water first and then
put his large suntanned hands, freshly rubbed on the soap
bar, over mine as if we were praying together. A giant's

hands. A towering giant bent down to spread gentleness over me like Ivory soap bubbles sliding over an afternoon's accumulation of grime.

"You kids stay out of that brooder house. Did you know that you left the door open? We could have lost all the chicks. Now stay out." The temper of his message was echoed in his quick, determined stride as he turned and left us standing on the porch. An adventure was foiled, but the stern command could not be questioned. No compromises. Mother was the one to be persuaded. Dad was to be listened to.

Dinner music, country style. The forks clink against the plates. Coffee mugs clunk as they are set down.
"Hon, get your father some more coffee."
He held up his cup as I began to pour, his bare arm extended. I was embarrassed by its nakedness and the strength that welled up in his forearm and biceps. I was amused, too, by the saddle-shoe tan that marks him a farmer just as surely as his calloused hands and bib overalls.
"Be careful. You're going to give him too much. That's it. Thanks."

"Margaret, where are those two? The chores haven't even been started. They know they're supposed to start them the minute they get home."
"I'll check, Kenneth. I'll check."
"Well, get them out here."
The edge on his voice was familiar. Whenever he had a headache his patience wore thin and it showed. But there was work to be done in the barns and we had our share. His strength fused with a respect for duty, and responsibility became our birthright. His demands on himself set the tone for our expectations of ourselves.

"It was a good crop this year, wasn't it?"
"Yes, and these steers should be ready for the market in another month. If it goes this well next year, we could have the land bank paid off. Then we can do the remodeling we've talked about."

He leaned against the gray board fence, his brown hair matted to his head by the cap he now held in his hands. His lean frame relaxed as he looked past the barns. Lost in thought, now, the lines becoming prominent around his mouth and eyes were softened by the luxury of a moment's dream.

The unbelievable happens in every family. Perhaps it was more unbelievable this time. She wasn't even two years old. My adolescent mind couldn't grasp the full meaning of death and I searched from one face to another, looking for a clue as to how to respond. He paced up and down the room, anger and frustration so compacted in him that his familiar, solid tread was growing unsteady with the burden of grief. "Why?" The frustration in that question that we all formed was flung up at some unseen enemy as his arm moved in a gesture of defiance. Then it dropped limply at his side. No words. Only love's capacity exposed in the capacity for hurt.

The arrangement of these episodes aids our understanding of the writer and her father. As the girl matures, she more clearly and more fully perceives the complexity of her father's character. She begins to understand him as a man of emotion as well as an authority figure. The sequential arrangement of the episodes reveals the growth of the girl and of her father.

Short episodes like these may lead you to write longer, more sustained descriptions of another person or of a relationship. When you begin to organize a longer, more extensive paper, you will want to control the central focus of the paper. For the purposes of discussion we can separate the matter of focus into three possible choices: you might focus mainly on the *person* you are writing about; you might focus primarily on your *relationship* to that person; or you might focus on your *response* to that person. All three possibilities are acceptable; none is inherently better than the others. The difference is in the writer's intent. When you wish to write about your relationship with another person, you can use any of the writing modes suggested later—direct description, dramatization, interview, and so on. But within that mode you will attend both to yourself and to the other person. The reader will learn about the part each of you plays in that relationship. When you focus on another person, the reader will learn more about the other person and less about you. When you focus on your responses to a person, the reader will learn more about you than about the person described.

These distinctions, of course, are arbitrary at best. A character sketch always establishes an implicit relationship between the writer and the person being described. The way you handle this implicit relationship will affect the focus of the writing. In most papers a writer will include all three possibilities. You may for example focus primarily on a person but also give some attention to your response to the person and your relationship with him or her.

Even some of the brief examples discussed earlier have a central focus. The physical descriptions of the woman in the waiting room and the young pregnant woman focus on a person. "Grandma Nellie" in Chapter 2 (p. 17) also focuses on a person. The selection from *Ulysses* in Chapter 3 (p. 44) emphasizes Molly's responses to other people. The two examples of conversation in this chapter give central emphasis to a relationship. The focus in "Pieces of a Portrait Found While Traveling through Childhood" is more evenly distributed, for the reader learns about the father, about the daughter, and about their relationship.

Whatever you choose to emphasize in your paper, you will want to make your decision consciously rather than by accident. As you read through the next paper, consider what the writer is emphasizing and in what ways she controls the focus of the paper.

TOM

The torn shades flapped listlessly at the window. I wondered vaguely how many times they had been replaced since 1892, the date on the building. Despite the heat, the children were working intently; the only sounds in the room were the soft scratchings of pencils, the occasional rustling of papers and the decisive click of the minute hand on the clock. Pop! The spell was broken by a muffled, familiar sound. All eyes turned immediately to the center back of the room.

Lowering his desk top warily, Tom peeked over, his eyes darting to the right and left, settling on the floor, finally rising to meet mine. The rest of his face emerged, most of the brown skin covered by a circular pink elastic blob. He barely controlled the crinkles starting in the corners of his eyes. I raised my eyebrows, awaiting explanation, barely controlling the corners of my mouth.

He rubbed his jaws with both hands, pulled the pink mess away, rolled it into a ball, and popped it back into his mouth. He shook his head and heaved a long, timed sigh. "Gum done exploded, Teachah," he said in a voice aproximating self-reproach. "Don't know why that company make such weak gum. Gotta write me a letter and explain to that company."

I shook my head to indicate I was more interested in the gum than the letter writing. "You know the school rules, Tom. Wrap the gum in paper and bring it up to the wastebasket."

He ducked behind his desk again, adjusting the top, with loud clashing of hinges to each of the four levels thoughtfully built in by the American Seating Company. Finding none of the adjustments satisfactory, he leaned the top against his nose, rolled his eyes toward the ceiling, and made halfhearted stirring motions in his desk, searching for scrap paper.

"Buscat, she waitin on y'all," Steve elbowed him.

"F . . g you, niggah," Tom hissed, eyes bulging open, mouth in a puffed pout. The class reacted gleefully to his mimicry of the white man's stereotype. They watched me. There were conventions regarding classroom obscenities that they expected me to uphold.

I bit my lips to keep down that smile. "Tom, I beg your pardon. Would you repeat that loud enough for all of us to hear?"

He switched to his wrinkled old ape-faced frown. He remembered to shuffle his feet a bit and he dangled his arms at his sides. "I just told Steve to forget his old raggety self, Teachah, and I can't find no paper since you helped me clean my desk." The frown crumpled and was transformed to a placating innocent Uncle Tom grin. He chewed his gum vigorously.

"OK. I'll get you some. Please bring up your arithmetic paper at the same time."

He grabbed his arithmetic paper, and dribbling an imaginary basketball he Meadow Larked his way straight into the oversized metal cabinet I used for library and storage.

"Blockin! Ain't you gonna call that cabinet for blockin', Teachah?" He scratched a bald spot on his head, one of the three he'd made while trying to cut his hair with clippers, and waited for justice.

"In about ten seconds I may be making some other calls, Tom."

"Score! Teachah score. Yea Teachah!" Darnell led the cheer as Tom, counting aloud, zoomed to the front of the room, just making the wastebasket on ten. I dismissed the rest of the class for recess.

Tom shoved the arithmetic paper at me. There were three problems at the left corner. The rest of the paper was filled with black count marks and a generous number of smudges as he had counted and recounted. He would not work in the special workbook I'd bought him. "Pretty good work. Huh, Teachah?" I nodded. He removed the gum from his mouth, slowly wrapped it in the scrap paper and let it roll from his hand to the basket. "Can I stay after school and wash boards, Teachah? I won't make drip marks and smears like GIRLS do. I wash boards good. Miz' Southwell taught me." I nodded permission. He grabbed his cap, sent over his shoulder a few bars of a husky, throaty "When the Saints Go Marching In," and lunged out the door a Louie Armstrong. Funny how that official notice on my desk said he was Special Ed.

In part, this paper is a sketch of Tom. The dramatization of his physical appearance, his language, and his humorous antics draw our immediate attention. Except for the final sentence, the author offers very little direct assessment of Tom. Instead she recreates a specific classroom encounter that dramatically and indirectly communicates Tom's uniqueness. The paper is more than a characterization of Tom, however. The teacher narrates the incident. Her response to Tom and his classmates shapes the tone and focus of the paper. She is amused by Tom ("I raised my eyebrows, awaiting explanation, barely controlling the corners of my mouth"), but she also maintains the authority role that the class expects of her ("There were conventions regarding classroom obscenities that they expected me to uphold"). She relates her entire interchange with Tom in a tone of humorous understanding. Her lively dramatization of Tom's mimicry and the reaction of the rest of the class indicate her ability to fully appreciate the situation. Without her sympathetic response, our reaction to Tom might be quite different. Though the encounter does indeed characterize Tom, the central focus of the paper is on the interchange—the relationship between Tom and the teacher.

We have been discussing and illustrating the variety of ways you can focus a paper. A second choice facing you when you begin writing about others is that of *direct* or *indirect characterization*. Direct characterization relies on expository statements, that is, the writer tells the reader about another person. The earlier examples of physical description (p. 83) and the sketch of grandpa (p. 88) illustrate direct characterization. Writers usually employ direct characterization when they are establishing a background for an incident or an experience that will be the focal point of the writing. But it is also possible to write an entire paper by directly describing a character. Direct characterization is easier for beginning writers because it allows them to use abstract labels and to summarize information about a person. You will want to experiment with both direct and indirect methods of describing people. Indirect characterization often relies on dramatization to communicate information about a person. When writers indirectly characterize someone, they usually provide sufficient information to lead their readers to the intended conclusions. The writer seldom offers direct evaluation of the character's motives, ability, or personality. In this way the reader is encouraged to participate in the process of responding, perceiving, and evaluating the person described. The previous sketch of Tom and his teacher, the two earlier examples of conversations (pp. 84 and 86), and "Pieces of a Portrait Found While Traveling Through Childhood" each rely heavily on indirect characterization, as does the short story "Jennifer" in Chapter 9 (p. 206). Most papers are a mixture of direct and indirect characterization.

At times you may want to write about your encounters with groups of people rather than about one person. This can be done in various ways. There are several possible focal points, just as there are when you write about one person. You can focus your attention on the group itself—perhaps writing about them in the third person; you can write about your encounters with the group —emphasizing the encounter; or you can write about your reactions to the group. Most of the time your writing will include all these elements.

When you write about your experiences with a group of people, you are moving out into an ever diversifying world. Just as in Whitman's poem "There Was a Child Went Forth," your world widens, diversifies, and becomes more complex as you move from single encounters with persons you know well to encounters with groups of people. The writing possibilities are varied. You might write about your encounter with an impersonal group of people, none of whom you knew—perhaps a crowd at an airport, or the crowd around you at a movie or sports event, perhaps a group of people gathered at a political rally. Or the writing might deal with more intimate and personal relationships to groups of people, such as a church retreat, an encounter group or group therapy, a club, or simply a group of friends you know well.

APPROPRIATE WRITING MODES

You may use any of the following modes to write about others.

narration or description

You might describe a person (from first person or from a more removed third person point of view) or a relationship; or you might narrate an incident that expresses a relationship or characterizes a person. The emphasis here is on talking about incidents or experiences rather than dramatizing those experiences. In description and narration the writer's presence is more obviously evident than in dramatization. In fact his or her attitudes, emotions, and thoughts are often the shaping force of the writing.

You might begin by relating an eye-witness account of an event, describing the details of what you see and experience. Later you can link together a series of events or encounters that have shaped or defined a relationship you have had with someone or that define a person for you. These writing experiences lead naturally toward fiction writing.

interview or dialogue

You might relate either informal or formal conversations. Here the emphasis is on talk and on how what we say helps to define us—how talk contributes to our character, or characterizes someone else. Also you will become aware of how talk shapes and defines your relationship with others.

There are several possible emphases to explore in this mode. You can begin by simply relating what two people actually say to each other in a given situation. (One possibility is for the class to break into pairs, with students recording what their partners have said. Or the participants could conduct more formal interviews, recording questions and answers.) Later you may decide to include references to setting (where the conversation took place) and the interviewer's personal response to what was said. As you begin to record interviews or conversations, you should include information about the thoughts, gestures, or facial expressions of either person. Such complete renditions of dialogue, setting, action, and character are, of course, moving in the direction of dramatization or fiction. If you wish, you might cast the conversation in the form of a story with dialogue.

Recording what is said in either a conversation or an interview alerts you to the importance of spoken language and what it contributes to your perceptions of others. It also helps you to perceive more clearly the relationship between what you feel, what you think, what you say, and how you respond to what others say to you.

dramatization

The emphasis in dramatization is on incident, action, or event as each reveals character. You could pick an event that delineates the character of a relationship and dramatize it for the reader. This might be done as a scene from a play or as a skit, or as a narrative or story that relies heavily on dialogue and action. (The narrative is, of course, subordinated to the action.) In dramatization all the previously mentioned modes can come into use. Drama attempts to demonstrate directly a character's personality or the workings of a relationship by what is said, what is done, and what is described. In drama there is little direct evidence of your personal opinion as a writer. Drama encourages you to observe and record how events and situation contribute to—perhaps even shape—your perceptions of and relationships to others.

SPECIFIC WRITING POSSIBILITIES

Record a conversation in class or elsewhere.

Create dialogue that might occur in a local place, for example, a dorm room, the student union, a bus, and so on.

Write a brief dialogue that you imagine would take place between the two people in an ad or a photograph.

Create a dialogue that takes place in response to a painting.

Write a character sketch of yourself in different roles and situations, or a sketch of yourself from another's point of view.

Write a character sketch, concentrating on the physical details of a stranger.

Write a character sketch, first indicating your initial reaction to or impression of the person (someone you do not know). Then cite the physical details that support your opinion. (The description will be a mixture of objectivity and subjectivity.)

In a character sketch, describe in detail someone you know but dislike. Try to influence the reader indirectly (no direct condemnation).

Compose a character sketch that describes someone who

seemed to be one sort of person but was finally revealed to be quite different.

Describe a person first in favorable terms and then from the opposite point of view. You could use yourself. How do you see yourself? How do others see you?

Describe someone very different from you. You might create a dialogue between you and the person.

Sympathetically characterize a person you disagree with or dislike.

In a character sketch, describe an aggressive, rebellious person or a shy, withdrawn person.

Describe a brief encounter, of any sort, between you and another person.

Dramatize a relationship with a person who strongly influenced your life, focusing on one or two significant incidents.

Write a diary entry from someone else's point of view.

Write a diary entry as it might be written by another person.

Describe or dramatize a close relationship you have had with another person. You might want to emphasize one or two specific encounters.

Write a character sketch that includes the character's inner thoughts as well as his or her external dialogue with others.

Recreate an encounter in which you failed to be friendly or sympathetic to someone who needed help.

Recreate either a situation in which you experienced a sense of belonging or community with other people or an incident when you felt out of place or uncomfortable in a group. Try to communicate how the experience influenced you.

Describe or dramatize an experience you had with a group of people (a protest group, sensitivity group, religious group, and so on) in which you learned about yourself, the other people, and the goals of the group.

shaping autobiography

At first glance the title of this chapter may confuse you, since nearly all the writing you have done so far has been in some sense autobiographical. You have already been examining and expressing your experience in the three previous chapters, but each time you have been focusing on one specific aspect of your experience—your encounters with yourself, with place, or with people. Though the specific topics of your papers have varied, in all these earlier writings you probably have been developing a more comprehensive understanding of your own life. You now may be better prepared to write about the significant events, experiences, or relationships of your life in a more sustained, coherent, and integrated manner. Instead of recording isolated images, unrelated memories, brief conversations, or descriptions of other people, you can try to organize a more extended and comprehensive paper that will convey significant insights about the complex relations you have experienced with things, places, and people.

I am not, however, asking you to communicate your entire life, nor do I expect a thorough exploration of large segments of your past. Certainly I am not speaking of autobiography in the conventional sense—the unrelenting documentation of facts and data that record your progress from birth to college. On the contrary, I would encourage you to be selective in your choice of material. The student papers that appear later in this chapter illustrate a variety of approaches. The writers concentrate on one specific incident ("I'm Afraid There's Been a Misunderstanding"), on a series of related incidents ("Margaret and I"), or on a situation or relationship ("My Blank Eyes" and "Ida Indecisive").

The challenge is a difficult one, for autobiography requires you to view your past with honesty, clarity, and a considerable degree of objectivity. You may in fact resist writing about your life, for reviewing past experience can sometimes be painful or distressing. It can also be intensely rewarding to write about your past, for by doing so you can revive and record significant moments in your life. Certainly I am not suggesting that you dredge up and express unpleasant experiences that you are unwilling to share. I am encouraging you, however, to write about an experience, a few incidents, or a relationship that you feel will characterize your life in some meaningful way.

Some student writers may feel they have little, if anything, to say about their lives; others will feel they have far too much to say to confine themselves to only one paper. Most of you will probably fall somewhere in between. More than likely, the earlier assignments and writing experiences in this book will have provided you with considerable material from which you can shape a more sustained autobiographical paper. You may, for example, decide to expand an earlier paper relating an emotional incident or describing a place. You may revise a previous description of a relationship. Perhaps a free association or a collection of childhood images you wrote in Chapter 3 has already suggested an appropriate autobiographical paper.

If the earlier writing experiences do not suggest a suitable topic for autobiography, you may want to write some journal entries or other preliminary sketches that will explore your past and revive your memories. Perhaps you could do a free association on your childhood summers, or you could simply try to recollect isolated memories that are in some way meaningful to you. You could begin by sketching a variety of attitudes, relationships, places, or experiences that have shaped your life. In the excerpt below, the writer sorts through a collection of her memories, trying to express her identity.

I've been trying to figure out what my life has added up to—which may be a bad place to begin. Better, maybe,
I should begin with what it is I am the sum total of.

When I was five I was in a ballet recital with my older sister. I wore a green chiffon costume with wings. Bonnie was good, but I was only five.

Fourth grade reading tests were a drag—and so I said on one such test question. Mrs. Palmer didn't consider me a qualified judge and scared me so much that any academic dissent I ever possessed was repressed for the next ten years—(or how to get to college).

My piano teacher from first grade on was Mrs. Potts. Celia Potts: sixty, five feet tall, a gray bun on top of her head, always maroon or gray knit dresses with her Supphose, and she had a nervous habit of moving her mouth like a kissy doll. Sixth grade was the first of my many performances at her Monday Historical Club. My mother called it the Monday Hysterical Club.

Seventh grade my first run-in with the police. One of my friends had an outdoor pajama party, and it was June. About 3:00 A.M. Cathy and I decided to take a stroll. It was so beautiful and so quiet outside, that suddenly we found ourselves downtown. In a town of 2,000, the only thing going on downtown at that hour is the traffic light—no people—no cars—just a traffic light going green yellow red. So until our tranquility was so rudely broken, we stood on the corner for a short while, gazing at the light, listening to the quiet, our long flannel nightgowns floating with the breeze . . .

I can see where I have become like some people I've known. But more evident to me are those people I have made a conscious effort to become unlike.

I really hated my sister. She was always screaming or crying, vomiting to make a point. One night she threatened to jump out her bedroom window with her ice skates on —which she did. At 17 she was married, at 18 a mother. At 20 she was divorced. I went from hating to pitying her. Now I think I can understand and accept her for what she forced herself into becoming. Even though I don't ever want to be anything resembling her, I can still love her— she's my sister.

It takes about two or three minutes to get to my

grandmother's from my house. It's a nice walk through a couple of backyards, past a few weeping willows, and into her garden. She was always there to study with, to eat with, to play the piano with, to communicate with, to be silent with. She taught me how to drive, and she taught me how to relax.

She went to see *Jesus Christ Superstar* at the University—in a field house. Falling up the bleachers, she sat among a few thousand joint-passers. ("You know, it smells like burning rags.") She's eighty—and I love and admire her more than anyone I've ever known.

This paper is not a coherent autobiography, but it does illustrate one way you might begin. The writer here is simply cataloguing a series of events that she feels represent her life. She makes no attempt to link events explicitly or to interpret their significance. Nor is there any attempt to give one or two events the central focus of the paper. If you can revive an assortment of memories like these, however, you may be able to select one or two of them for a more extensive treatment.

Another preliminary writing experience that may lead to an autobiographical paper is a description of yourself as you are now—your hopes, fears, problems, or relationships with others. By struggling to communicate these matters candidly, you will probably touch on significant moments or influences from your past. You might then examine those influences more closely to see if you can find a topic that will link your past experiences to your present life. At first you may have difficulty being candid with yourself and your reader. Notice how rambling and disconnected the focus is in the following paper, "Brown Shoes and Tuxedos"; it reads like a hesitant journal entry. The writer does not always choose his words carefully, nor does he seem to know what the intent of his paper is. After wrestling with the opening paragraphs, the writer finally admits his fear of exposure—and his reluctance to be honest about his feelings and experiences. Yet once he admits his fear, it no longer is an insurmountable obstacle. The second half of the paper candidly attempts to communicate the writer's attitudes and experiences. He begins to express more specifically his sense of being somehow out of place in college.

BROWN SHOES AND TUXEDOS

I took a walk into the valley today (tonight rather)—I really didn't know before but we've got a tiny forest down there. When it's real quiet and you listen hard enough you can hear the manyness of trees straining from the ice that is covering every one of them. It rained all day covering everything in ice because it also happened to be un-hot at the same time. If you listen hard enough, in fact, the crackling of the ice-covered trees can become quite loud. I've heard different opinions about today: "If it weren't so cold it wouldn't be so bad." "Isn't it pretty?" "This day is for shit."

Why is everything bad happening to me lately? I'm not exaggerating. I've been watching the walls close in on me. I feel like the old Edsel I saw at the scrap yards being de-larged because nobody liked it any more (maybe nobody ever liked it). Maybe someday that old Edsel will be reborn into a beautiful specimen of steel, rubber, and chrome; one that everyone (or at least SOMEBODY) will like. I hope in some way that will happen to me someday. Crosby, Stills, Nash, and Young are doing an un-bad job of inspiring me right now;

> "It's getting to the point where I'm
>   no fun any more.
> I am sorry.
> Sometimes it hurts so badly I must cry
>   out loud—
> I am lonely."[1]

I don't know if I'm going to last thru this semester the way my classes are going. That is another thing that is bothering me. Then there is the problems I share with certain members of my family back home.

> "I've got an answer, I'm going to fly
>   away. What have I got to lose?

[1] "You Make It Hard," from "Suite: Judy Blue Eyes," words and music by Stephen Stills. © 1969 Gold Hill Music, Inc. P.O. Box 44282, Panorama, Calif. 91402. All rights reserved. Used with permission.

Will you come see me Thursdays and
Saturdays? What have you got to
lose?"[2]

Didn't think you would.

I can't think of anything more to write about and I
know this work has to be two pages typewritten, single
spaced so from here on I'm just gonna write what comes
into my head whether it makes sense or not. Truth is
there is a lot I could write about but I don't have the guts
for fear that someone may find out to whom this masterpiece
belongs. I'm a pilot (a student pilot) or at least I'm trying
to be one. I enjoy it a hell of a lot but it hasn't changed me
at all. I thought it would. When I'm up there I do feel different
especially when I'm flying around alone and my instructor
isn't with me. When I climb to altitude, I am alone. There
is no sign of life looking down from 9,000 feet. The only
way I know there's life being led down there is the radio
reminding me of that fact. Sometimes I even turn that off.
It's stranger than hell. Up there I enjoy being alone—I get a
charge out of it. On a clear day I can see into tomorrow
and I get a kick out of that too. But, what goes up must
come down. I'm still alone and I don't like it as much.
And sometimes I look forward to tomorrow. I've given it
some thought. I used to wish that what's his name never
got that headache when the proverbial apple fell on his
head. I used to wish that I could take off and not come down
again. But I know I would only get tired of that after a
while.

I'm also different when I've tipped a few beers. It's
beautiful. I don't have to get drunk mind you—just a few
beers. I can talk then. I've got plenty (not too much) to say.
That's what is causing my under-par social life. I'm a lousy
conversationalist. I was brought up differently from most
kids. My folks are from the old country. But now that I
think about it, that couldn't be the cause of it. I had plenty

[2] "You Make It Hard," from "Suite: Judy Blue Eyes," words and music by
Stephen Stills. © 1969 Gold Hill Music, Inc. P.O. Box 44282, Panorama,
Calif. 91402. All rights reserved. Used with permission.

of friends when I was a kid and I considered myself to be Joe American. But something happened. My God, I was born and raised in this country but somewhere along the line I missed something. Maybe it was because I never watched Captain Kangaroo or something like that. I feel the same way in some of my classes. They are supposed to be introductory classes but I swear I feel as though I missed something. I loved Popeye. He was cool. I was an altar boy, a paper boy, a safety boy, a Boy Scout (a patrol leader no less) and an all around weirdo. Wow my mood just made a 180 degree turn. I was feeling lower than Mickey Rooney in the Grand Canyon when I started this paper last night and it carried on till just now. I'm not bullshitting you either. Tis true. I'm not always in a bad mood—don't get the wrong idea. Something happened late last night. My love life took another nose-dive. So I started this paper to get my mind off it. It's a good thing I did or I never would have gotten it finished in time. All I need is some black polish. That will take care of my brown shoes. All I need is a little time. I've never even thought of giving up yet. There is hope for me yet. Just remember the famous words of President McKinley . . . . . what did he say??? Catch ya later.

This paper is far from a polished, sustained autobiography, but it does demonstrate how painful autobiographical writing can be. Only in the last two paragraphs does the writer openly discuss his life. His candid, personal voice finally breaks through, despite the paper's lack of concrete details and precise language. This preliminary writing experience has helped him discover and express the basic attitudes that characterize his life. In the final paragraphs he talks about his feelings and touches on an assortment of memories that he feels are significant. He emphasizes his inability to communicate and his sense of not belonging, and he begins to suggest specific reasons for his present emotional state. By the end of the paper he has identified some central concerns, which he might explore more extensively in his next draft. Though "Brown Shoes and Tuxedos" needs considerable revision as an autobiography, it does underscore the importance of viewing your life candidly and communicating opinions or experiences that you feel are significant.

As you select the specific content of your paper, you will want to be sure you have sufficient emotional or chronological distance to interpret your experience clearly. When you write about your own life, you usually need to develop a dual perspective—that is, you must be both "in" and "out" of your past experience. You will want to render the experience with enough detail or dramatic immediacy to make it real for your reader. At the same time, you will want to keep enough emotional distance from the experience to be able to give it an organization and clarity that convey an understanding of the experience. The writer must be able both to recreate and to assess the experience. Sometimes it is possible to think of autobiographical writing as having two narrators—a younger self who experiences the event or relationship, and an older self who narrates that experience and who by the organization, emphasis, and tone demonstrates an understanding of that experience.

Since it is usually difficult to assess experiences fully at the time they are happening, you may want to avoid dealing with recent or current events in your life. It may be more productive to focus on a past experience that you can view with greater perspective and a fuller understanding.

In the autobiographical sketch below the writer's dual perspective is most evident in the opening four paragraphs.

Margaret and I served time together in our youth—eight years of incarceration in the revered Roman Catholic educational system available to families in our neighborhood. Early in our confinement the nuns owned us: mind, body, and soul—beany cap, prayer book, and rosary. We were devout in those days, though Margaret was better at it than myself. As she glided toward the communion rail her fingers, with her $7.50 rosary draped through them at a most reverent angle, pointed straight to heaven in an exact emulation of Sister Agnes Marie. Margaret's mom taught at the school—she was holier than both of us combined. She moved on the elevated level with the nuns. I think her rosary cost $13.50. Margaret let me hold it once and by the hallowed texture of the beads I could tell that her mother would be a saint.

I, of course, had the prescribed milk-white-just-for-our-girls-$1.04-holy-blessed-rosary. My mother had never been convinced that the sanctity of the prayer was infinitely multiplied by the quality of the rosary. My zeal was also somewhat hampered by the standard brown-toned illustrations in my prayer book. In Margaret's edition the glory of God shone in full color. She was generous though and, in the goodness of grace that the book imparted to her, she let me read it at least once a week. When I got my glasses and could see the pictures while sitting beside her, we shared the book and were equally blessed.

Whole families of wide-eyed believers were sent to the school to be molded into obedient servants of the Church. According to tradition, it is expected that when the benevolent God sends—however mysteriously—His gifts, the recipient family should return at least a few of them as proof of their true Christian spirit and lack of avarice. The method of return most favored by God is, of course, that of monetary return on each and every Sunday. Excluding that—a twenty-five-cent gift per week does not leave much to return—the next most gallant offering is that of a child. As the chest-stabbing days of Abraham were definitely considered passé, the Church had devised an alternate method by which the gift can dedicate herself forever to the service of the Almighty. As added incentive, the method included a floor-length black robe and the right to be called "Sister."

Both Margaret's family and my own attended the school, and no one in either family showed any indication of offering himself for transformation to the holy state. Margaret and I knew within the very souls of our sparse bosoms that we were the Chosen ones. We resigned ourselves to our mutual fate and began to practice works of charity, such as helping the nuns after school.

But in the spring of our fourth year with the nuns I realized that beneath the long black skirts of their habits, the sisters had feet of clay. Ironically enough, it was

Margaret's mom who brought me to this knowledge. She was the first of the exalted to topple from the pedestal of the holy ones to the mundane pettiness of mortals. From spring until summer, Margaret's mother relentlessly kept my brother after classes. She forced him to practice penmanship while the shrieks of the softball game rose from the field below.

I'd see him when I passed by the room on my way to pound erasers. For a moment I'd stand beside the door, clutching chalky erasers and sneezing in their dust. He'd look up then and contort his face into an expression that mimicked the crucifix on the classroom wall. Teeth still clenched in mock agony of the divine, one eye would open and wink. I'd smile and then move on to the next room's erasers.

He never completed the extra assignments; he just sat there in the gold glow of the afternoon sun and struggled to control the wandering pencil. Because they locked the school at five o'clock she would have to let him leave. But by then the game was over and we had to hurry home to dinner. My brother never complained to her, but on his calendar he marked off each day until summer.

Throughout the summers, my brother used to collect grasshoppers—the shiny green ones that hop on you when you lay in the tall grass. He'd lay there for hours, out on the hill behind our house; on his back with his long legs bent in a V, his head propped on the lawn mower, waiting for grasshoppers to jump on him. While he laid there squinting in the sun, there was a song he used to sing. It was about the lazy grasshopper who played a fiddle instead of working. In my brother's version, though, the grasshopper wasn't really lazy. He just fiddled because he loved music. The ants never understood how the grasshopper could be content to fiddle day after day, but they helped him in the end. My brother said that the ants will always help him, even when they believe he is lazy, because his music makes their life beautiful.

We still sing the grasshopper song when my brother stops home for a visit. I even found a copy of the grasshopper

fable and mailed it to him for his twentieth birthday.
He should have gotten it by now—if he's still living at the
same address. Although he moves a lot, wherever he goes
he lives in summer. Margaret and I are going to Florida
next week to visit him. We've grown weary of the winter's
work and Margaret is eager for a glimpse of summer.
This will be my turn to let her touch the beauty of my
$13.50 rosary; to let another person be charmed by the
summer grasshopper's melodies of love.

For me, summer was always a time of peace and
wondering, a time for nature and farms. I stayed several
days with my cousins on their farm in the summer before
I turned seven. We played hide and seek in the corn field,
and for the first time, I saw a mouse. The mouse was
strange and evil—mice bite you and you die—so I ran
from it. We swung with a rope too; high up to the barnloft
where we laid in the piled hay and listened to the humming
of the insects.

On the last day of my visit, my father's family gathered
on the farm for a glorious Sunday afternoon picnic. The
aunts brought baskets of food, checkered tablecloths, and
lemonade. The uncles consulted, argued, and finally agreed
on the best method for making ice cream. My cousins
and I played tag and took turns at cranking the ice cream
freezer. There were so many of us that no one missed
my cousin Caroline until we were all seated at the tables
to eat. Caro and I were close in age and she usually sat
beside me. Her brother was sent to find her. When he finally
returned, I had finished my dinner and was idly spitting
watermelon seeds into a zinnia patch. Replete and satiated,
I imagined myself swallowed by the pulsating sun and
was deliciously aware of the idyll that was summer.

Caro's brother had been unable to find her; his father
left to help him search. I was aiming the seeds at a large
red zinnia in the middle of the patch when I saw my cousin
return—this time, his face convulsed hideously, screaming
for his mother. Daddy reached him first and grabbed him
roughly by the shoulders. Then they turned and ran
toward the barn, followed closely by the rest of my uncles.

Mom gathered the children and forced them to play quietly in the backyard. I crouched in the zinnias along the drive and was not noticed. The mellow, mute voices had changed to sobs and screaming tears; not even the sun could warm me now. The county ambulance came hustling up the drive and Caro's mother screamed at the attendants to hurry. But my uncle walked slowly up from the barn then, stumbling and blind with tears, gently cradling the gray blanketed bundle that had been Caro. The attendants were ready with their equipment but they did not use it after they had unwrapped her. Huddled in the sickening sweetness of the zinnias, I saw the pale gold curls and the dark frightened face of my strangled cousin. The marks from the hayloft's "swingin' rope" still twisted themselves into her neck.

Mom found me shivering in the zinnias a few hours later—alone in the dusky shadows—too afraid to leave. She gathered me close into the warmth of her arms, and her tears slipped gently down my face.

The three sections of this paper are not as effectively integrated as they might be. In fact, some readers feel the essay is really three separate, loosely connected papers. Despite this weakness, however, the paper is indeed interesting because it does include a variety of writing styles and tones. The first section, describing the writer's early religious training, is controlled by the satirically humorous point of view. We learn directly about the younger girl and indirectly about the older writer. The second section focuses on the writer's relationship with her brother. The satiric tone is replaced by a warm, approving tone. She refers to her brother as her $13.50 rosary, thus suggesting his philosophy as a viable alternative to a religious approach to life. In the third section, once again the tone and mode changes. This section dramatizes the childhood memory of her cousin's accidental death. As is usual in dramatization, the narrative voice is considerably removed. The writer recreates the events as vividly as possible and refrains from the kind of editorial commentary and opinion that permeates the opening section. The tone of this last section is serious, and the impact is forceful.

As an example of an autobiographical sketch, the paper serves to illustrate what I mean by a dual perspective and an integration of experience. The first section does achieve both of these, but the paper as a whole does not sustain that perspective and integration. The connection, for instance, between the death of the cousin and the other two sections is not as clear as it might be, especially since the chronological order of events becomes blurred. We can guess of course that the writer might be trying to say that it was the lack of explanation for the cousin's death that eventually turned her away from religion toward her brother's philosophy, but this connection is not clearly established. In spite of these defects, however, the paper holds our attention. It is evident that the writer is intensely interested in the experiences and wants us to find them interesting too.

Earlier I suggested that you might choose to dramatize a relationship or an emotionally intense incident for your auto-biography. Each of the following papers vividly recreates a specific experience. Both writers carefully observe details and effectively use setting to reinforce the tone of the writing. The second paper relies much more heavily on the narrator's inner language. Though both writers integrate the narrator's internal reactions and observa-tions, the second paper relies more heavily on interior monologue. Notice too that the narrator in the first paper never comments directly on the emotional impact of her experience. She recon-structs the incident in sufficient detail for us to share the experi-ence and draw the intended conclusions. The narrator in the second paper expresses her feelings more explicitly; she more thoroughly explores her attitudes and behavior.

I'M AFRAID THERE'S BEEN A MISUNDERSTANDING

I looked down at the envelope with the address scribbled quickly in red. Yes, this is it, I thought. And to stave off my insecurity, I looked back again at the large plate glass window with the gold letters V.F.W. printed on it. Oh yes, Veterans of Foreign Wars. A quick panoramic view through the slats of the half-closed Venetian blinds revealed row upon row of dull grey, metal desks. There must have been at least twenty, all in neat, straight rows. At most of them sat sad, business-looking men who were either talking on the phone or writing on legal-sized pads of paper. I took one last long look at the glass window surface, now a convenient mirror, to check my lipstick supply and hairdo. it reflected a neat bouffant style hairdo framing a thin, youthful face of sixteen years. I rubbed my lips together, back and forth a couple of times, feeling the greasy oil of lipstick slide around. Satisfied, my chest heaved, resided, and I turned for the door.

Just inside to the right was a desk like all the others, but on the front was a cardboard name plate reading— Miss Clark, Receptionist. I cautiously walked toward the desk just as she mechanically turned her head from the ancient typewriter, smiled, and asked, "May I help you?" My hands fumbled with the envelope and my quiet voice responded for me with, "Yes, please. My high school counselor called down here for me . . . to see someone about money I have coming for me to go to college."

She nodded understandingly, picked up the phone, and pushed a lighted button. As she began to relate the information to the person on the other end, I thought about how I had explained my situation to her. I was a little disappointed in it as I had rehearsed what I was going to say all the way down to Detroit on the bus. After all, I wanted to make a good impression and express myself clearly and concisely like my speech teacher had taught us. I consoled myself with the rationalization that she was only the secretary and didn't count anyway. She wasn't giving me the money. My private thoughts stopped as she laid down the phone and said, "Yes, Miss Brady, Mr. Stimson will see you shortly. Please have a seat."

I sat down next to her desk. She went back to her typing and I went back to my own thoughts. I gazed around the cold, large room with no pictures on the walls. I twisted to get more comfortable, and in turning noticed a large crack in the far corner. This place was really in bad shape. They ought to give a little less money to kids for college and spend some in fixing up this place. I was thinking that I was sorry for the secretary for having to work in such a place when she interrupted with, "OK, Mr. Stimson can see you now. His desk is the last one in that last row." She uttered the instructions as she pointed.

As I confidently strode toward his row, I made a mental note that I would certainly explain my situation better to this Mr. Stimson. My high school counselor had told me that because my father had been killed in the war, I was entitled, as his orphan, to collect so much money for college expenses. And the fact that my mother had remarried a man who earned $20,000 yearly didn't matter. It was a good thing too. Just as I reached his desk, I felt a pang of guilt for not telling my mother I was coming down here. But then I thought—bitterly—angrily—why should I? Every time I did one little thing wrong, like forgetting to take out the garbage or coming home fifteen minutes late, my stepfather threatened me with, "Well, I'm not giving any money to a goddamned dumb jackass like you to go to college. Get the hell out of here. You make me sick." Each word slowly grinded out of his mouth like he was crushing me into oblivion with each one. And my mother? She never said a word. I was an honor student, with high principles, with high motivation. The hell with him, I had decided. Chuck you, Farley! I'll get my own money for college. I am entitled to it. I'll show you you don't have hold of all the strings that make me jump.

My angry mental war halted as Mr. Stimson extended his large, warm, strong hand for me to shake. He looked about forty years old but was very trim and even a bit on the handsome side.

"Won't you sit down?" he asked kindly.

"Yes, thank you," I answered sincerely, as I sat down and plopped my purse on the tile floor.

He quickly glanced down at a sheet of paper on his desk and unconsciously drummed a pencil on a giant-sized, joke-type, pink eraser. With a final rap of the pencil he began.

"Well, now, what was your father's name?" he questioned.

"Gerald Groves," I responded articulately, and he wrote it down on a little pad of paper, checking the spelling as he wrote.

"Now, what was his selective service number?"

I hesitated for a moment like a kid in school who knows he doesn't have the answer. "I'm sorry, but I don't know. I haven't seen him since I was a little baby and my mother won't talk about him at all. You can understand." I waited, sensing my answer wasn't enough.

"Well, hum . . ." Mr. Stimson muttered slowly, meditatingly, while he stroked his chin with index finger and thumb. I felt all my hopes and plans dashed forever. He must have noticed my look of despair because he perked up with, "But, we'll give it a try." He confidently picked up the phone, waited a moment, gave the facts to someone upstairs, and put down the receiver. He began asking me questions about what I wanted to study in college and where I was from. The kind of questions that kill time. But I think he was really interested too. Shortly, a man, much older and duller than Mr. Stimson, emerged from the elevator carrying a manila folder. He walked toward us, quietly laid it on the desk, and just as quietly walked back to the elevator as Mr. Stimson perfunctorily thanked him.

He opened the folder and quietly leafed through the pages of endless government forms. He made notes out loud. "Yes, everything is here." "Mr. Groves had entered the service on such and such a date and had been given an honorable discharge. No problem there. And, yes, he had married a Thelma Thomas in 1941." Things seemed to be going smoothly. Just then he jerked back his head as he began reading the first sheet of what looked like a many-paged document. I couldn't see what it was, but I wondered because Mr. Stimson wrinkled up his forehead and squinted his eyes.

"Is something wrong?" I asked hesitantly.

He looked me straight in the eyes. He was very serious.

"Your . . . your father didn't die in the war, Miss Brady.

Your parents were divorced a year after the war." He
didn't seem to know what to say next or if he should have
even said what he had said.

"But . . . why?" I asked.

He explained as nicely as he could that he just
wasn't allowed to divulge personal details from records,
but he finally admitted that the reason for the divorce read
"mental cruelty." I was still shocked, stunned, and confused.
What does mental cruelty mean, I wondered. A hard
lump lodged in my narrow throat. My heart beat through
every part of my body. I must keep composed, I thought.
I don't want to look silly or make a scene. Mr. Stimson
finally said simply, ever so simply, "Gee, I'm sorry to tell
you all this . . . this way, I mean. I guess there's been a
misunderstanding." I giggled back, in a way one does when
he is trying to hide his fear or anxiety, "Yes, I guess there
has been a misunderstanding. Thank you, anyway, for
your help." I said it with half a smile, then turned, rose,
and with hurried steps headed for the door, repeating the
meaningless words to my mind—I guess there's been
a misunderstanding.

AUTOBIOGRAPHY

My blank eyes wearily scanned the four walls of the
one-room apartment. Expressionless. Unseeing. Deliberately.
I focused them on an abstract painting opposite the olive
studio couch upon which I lay. Supported by a dark
mahogany bureau, the picture depicted an emaciated sailboat
resting on the last of her high mighty haunches. I wondered
why the picture was not hanging from the wall as pictures
should be. Slowly, the artist's painstakingly careful strokes
and lines dissolved into a whirling kaleidoscope of browns
and whites. I no longer saw, nor did I want to. I closed
my eyes and felt a cold thickness settle heavily in my
feet and hands. I knew if I were to look at them I would see
the pulsations of an intricate pattern of throbbing blue
lace. Just like years ago when I took ballet lessons from
a Mrs. Brock. I was very young at the time, no older than

five or six, and terribly self-conscious and shy. I wore a black leotard that emphasized the pale purpleness of my legs. The other girls' legs were full and flushed with a healthy tinge of pink. Mine were cold blue. Poor circulation? I really don't think so. But who wants purple legs or knobby knees or long, golden braids when high teased hair is the fashion? In sixth grade we had square dancing. Every now and then the girls had to ask the boys. I asked a certain Jeff Peterson. He abruptly and quite loudly refused. Horribly embarrassing. Funny that I should remember him now. He moved shortly after, and I never saw him again.

Slowly, almost painfully I forced my thoughts back to the present. Jason's apartment. One large room, a stereo and four hundred classical albums. The faint smell of chicken livers. Steady drip-drip gurgle of the radiator. Ah, yes, the present. Always the present. Jason cold and distant, his right arm around my waist like a heavy, dead weight. My scorched mind searching frantically for a reply to his rather unusual proposition of ten minutes ago. I had nothing to say, I felt nothing. Just this damnable dullness. I retained my cramped position, knees drawn upward, right arm underneath my breast. I kept my arm there for a reason. My left breast tended to droop and looked insignificantly small without its support. This way it appeared to have a little cleavage. Not much but definitely some. And with the emphasis placed on the bust today I wondered if he knew the reason why I kept my arm there. His words ran tormentingly through my mind.

"Ellen," he had said, his voice dry, matter of fact, "These incomplete sex acts we have shared have led to a certain unhappiness within me. Now just as I wouldn't want you to be unhappy, you shouldn't want me to be. Therefore, unless you agree to have intercourse with me, I'm afraid that I will resist all temptations, even when I'm lonely, and never call you again."

I had known this was coming. It didn't really surprise me. And so what was there to say? If I had asked why it was so important to him to have this "complete" relationship, he would have asked why it was so important to me that I wouldn't? And what could I say? Nothing, really. Yes, he certainly had an answer for everything. But maybe that comes with being Jason. Selfish, implacable, strong.

The silence was heavy and electric with tension. Upstairs, a loud thud. People. Movement. Life. We were frozen in our silences, like moths against a windowsill.

He broke the stillness. Perhaps he was tired and wished to be rid of my troublesome presence.

"Well," he said in his New York accent, "Haven't you anything to say"?

Anything to say, I thought. No, not really. Not anything to say. I pondered over the possibility that his accent was phony. False. Fake. How terrible if it was. Of course he had grown up in Queens, New York, but still it seemed a trifle too obvious, almost like he wanted to make damn well sure that I knew he had grown up in Queens. Though, I can't see why. Maybe I can, though. There's a certain status involved in being from out of state. It tends to elevate in the eyes of others one's level of material wealth and worldliness. Tuition, travel expenses, sophistication gained from those very travels. Perhaps that is why. When I was younger I used to love putting people on. Acting a part. Being a part. I was quite adept at it. I had a favorite story I especially enjoyed telling. About how my parents died, leaving me an orphan at the age of five in Wales. I was sent from Wales to America to live with distant relatives who were terrible. They feigned a kindness I was immediately able to see through. However, their kindness didn't last for long, I would tell my rapt listeners, because soon they did away with their pretenses and when they felt like hitting me they damn well hit me. I would then somewhat dramatically point out a scar directly below my left temple. (Actually I had fallen from a tree fort when I was little and hit my head on a sharp rock.) But it was fun, and the imitation I was able to give of Hayley Mills' British accent proved most convincing. Sometimes I felt sorry for those that believed me. How stupid of them.

Another impatient "Well?" from Jason brought me back to the still unanswered question. Something to say. Anything to say.

I muttered in a barely audible voice that I thought it was too bad.

"Yes, yes," he agreed, "too bad, too very bad."

Silence.

"Haven't you anything else to say?"

I shrugged my shoulders and tilted my brows upward. Like Scarlett O'Hara. I must think of something to say. Jason placed such a strong emphasis on keenness of the mind. M.S.U. is second rate. Nonintellectual. And so on. Shortly after meeting him I had run to the Student Book Store and purchased Margaret Mead's *Growing Up in New Guinea.* With supreme effort and concentration I managed to read twenty-five pages in the span of two weeks. However, I devoured *Gone with the Wind* in a day. A fair indicator of the line and intensity of my intellectual aspirations. Once I heard him remark to his friend Alan that he would take beauty over brains any day, on the assumption that intellect could be easily cultivated, whereas beauty was somewhat more difficult. A comforting thought.

Oh, God, I must say something. Anything. Unconsciously, I had been preparing a smart little speech intended to set him back a few paces. I sat up and in a moderately sarcastic tone said, "Jason, you being such a strong person, how could you possibly even like a person who conceded to your every demand? I couldn't. Eventually I'd despise that person. And besides, any decision I make I must be completely happy with. Very important to be happy with yourself. Perhaps not satisfied, but happy. Your cut and dried manner of seeing things really amazes me. That it's going to be either 'this' or 'nothing'."

I stared at him, the right amount of wonder tempered with the right amount of disgust. He stared back. His eyes were dark, but a faint gleam of admiration betrayed itself. Had I done right? I really didn't think so. I wasn't that happy. I looked at him. The deep-set brown eyes, the thin colorless lips, the mass of dark hair tumbling across his broad, tanned forehead, the prominent nose, rising and sharply descending in a thin straight line, and high cheekbones. I want to marry a man with high cheekbones. They are something I want my children to have: high, proud, insolent bones. I'm not sure why, but they remind me of suffering, and suffering makes people interesting. Where have I heard that before? Oh well, it doesn't matter, it's true enough. Look at all our great artists. Van Gogh. Michelangelo. They all suffered. And they all had high cheekbones too. But I haven't suffered, except perhaps from the comforts of middle-class life, and I'm not dull. But then again I have relatively high cheekbones. I don't think I could possibly marry a man unless he had high cheekbones, and I'd never marry Jason, and he's the only man I've dated that had had them. Jason is too particular. That's why I could never marry him. Of course, this very idiosyncrasy intrigues me. But how long could I live with it? Right now it's a game, I'm playing a part. But how would I ever be able to live with someone who insists on folding a bath towel so that the label doesn't show?

Again I looked at Jason. He viewed me in a detached manner. Slowly he arose from the couch and began dressing. A wave of humiliation swept over me. Oh, the absurdity of it all! My sitting naked on the couch while he. . . . Cat-like, I sprang off the couch and hastily threw on my clothes, neglecting a button here and there, stuffing my nylons into the pockets of my skirt. I withdrew my coat from the closet, determined to leave before he did. In a composed, disinterested voice I sang out an indifferent "Goodnight and goodbye," opened the door to the hallway and left.

"Wait a minute," he called after me, "where are you going?" His voice sounded cold and strange in the softly lighted corridor.

"To the dorm. I'm walking." Suddenly and for reasons I didn't understand I felt a large lump swell in my throat. I was going to cry and, oh God, I didn't want to do that. I hastened my steps. Brusquely he grabbed my arms and forced me inside the room.

"I want to walk," I said in a slight, quivering voice.
I felt smothered and desperately wanted to get away.
His hands were painful against my arms. "I'll drive you. It's
too late for you to walk. I'd worry."

The irony of his last statement caused my concealed
anger to erupt in an outpouring of loud, gulping sobs.
Angrily, I tore away from him and locked myself in the
darkness of the bathroom. Worry, I fumed, he didn't give
a damn. Frustration at my helplessness against the cool
power of his mind gave vent to huge, heaving sobs.
Yes, he'd have the last word. He'd drive me home. Damn him.
Suddenly my grief went beyond my initial anger and I felt
so very alone. I sank to the floor, the tiles, cool and
soothing, on my hot, wet face. Oh God, I thought, no one
cares. Not really. And nothing matters either. My
virginity, college, earning a degree. Nothing—nothing at
all. Nothing, because even what I do have doesn't mean
a goddamn to me. Something, please matter. And Jason,
he never cared. What a fool I was to think so. What if I
should kill myself? Wouldn't that be a twist. Razor blades
and red, red blood. I grimaced at my dramatics. Oh Christ,
Ellen. A story he had once told me about a woman who
found that her husband was cheating on her. Upon realizing
this, she slit her wrists, died, and her husband got the
woman anyhow. I smiled a sick smile, ashamed at my
silly performance. Wearily, I arose and faced myself in the
mirror of the medicine cabinet. Dribbles of gray mascara
streaked my tear-worn face, while two dark smudges
encircled my bloodshot eyes. My lips were a violet shade
of red, slightly parted and noticeably swollen. An ugly
red mark caused from the separations in the tiles creased
my cheek. What a mess. Carefully I wiped away the
mascara with a piece of wetted Kleenex and then applied
a cool damp washcloth to my forehead. Once again, the
silence. I wondered what Jason was doing. A sudden thought
struck me. Something mattered. These very tears I was so
diligently wiping away. They mattered. Ironically, even
Jason mattered. The first person in so long. He had excited
in me an emotion I thought long ago dead. He had hurt me.

123

My defenses weren't so strong after all. My increasing insensitivity to people, things, myself. Oh God, it felt good to cry, to be hurt. I unlocked the door and stepped out. Jason stood firmly planted in front of the doorway, his broad shoulders drawn back, his face unreadable. He opened the door and, with a gesture for me to follow, stepped out. I stole a last final glance at apartment 4-A, and, not completely believing I would never see it again, meekly followed him. The ride to the dorm was silent, the tension considerably lessened by my new frame of mind. He parked the car in front of the steps and left the motor running. A brief pause. He looked at me and in a sincere voice said, "Take care of yourself." I opened the car door and wordlessly stepped out. Slowly I walked up the smooth steps to the dorm. On the fifth step I spotted a red wool mitten. He was still watching me. Probably would till I went inside. I stooped over and picked it up. The buzzer rang, and the girl at the desk let me in. I handed her the mitten and hurried to my room. Inside the room I turned on the night light and lay down on the bed. I felt a strange peace. I knew what I was going to do, and I knew that it mattered.

A week passed. I was still sure. Certain of myself. Thursday night I picked up the telephone receiver and slowly dialed the number of apartment 4-A. I was happy. He mattered.

Both of these papers focus on a specific incident occurring in a particular location for a limited period of time. We can directly observe each writer's ability to speak to and relate with other people. We also learn a great deal about each narrator's inner thoughts and feelings.

In the first paper we learn that Miss Brady is bright, self-motivated, and independent. Since her stepfather abuses her, she is determined to finance her college education without his assistance. She travels alone to Detroit to apply for the scholarship without telling even her mother. Though she is at times insecure, she handles the entire incident with self-control and maturity. The paper deals with a highly charged emotional moment in the narrator's life—a moment when for the first time she learns that, contrary to what her mother has led her to believe, her father is not dead. Despite the strong emotional appeal, however, the writing does not become explicitly sentimental or self-indulgent. The girl is sufficiently detached from the incident to control the tone and organization of the paper. Both the writing and the narrator's behavior are restrained. The narrator does not need to state her feelings directly. She observes specific details about the office, the secretary, and Mr. Stimson. Because she has so vividly recreated the incident we are at least partially able to share her confusion, embarrassment, and shock.

The narrator in the second paper more directly shares her emotional responses with the reader. Though the situation is dramatic and includes some dialogue, the paper is dominated by the narrator's interior language. She shares with us her experiences with Jason as well as her memories of Mrs. Brock's dance class and of Jeff Peterson's refusal; she shares her present embarrassment, insecurity, and shortcomings; she shares her childhood pranks and fantasies. She even shares her melodramatic reactions.

The paper includes a combination of tenses, which are intended to distinguish the narrative voices; but at times these voices are difficult to separate. First there is the voice of the older girl, who looks back on her experience with Jason and recalls the details of one specific incident. She organizes the paper and selects the language and details. Then there is the younger girl, who is experiencing the emotional stress of the specific encounter in Jason's apartment. Sometimes she speaks in the present tense ("I must think of something to say." "I want to marry a man with high cheekbones"). She is at times melodramatic and superficial. At one point she says she has never suffered; she complains that nothing matters to her. At other times she is self-perceptive, grimacing at her own dramatics and admitting she is ashamed of her "silly performance." She is also able to recall her childhood behavior with an honest perspective.

The occasional use of the present tense is confusing, because we are not always sure if the thoughts should be attributed to the older girl or the younger girl. In the opening paragraph, for example, which voice asks "Poor circulation?"? It could be either voice. Perhaps some of the shifting of tenses occurs because the older narrator is still too close in time and emotional perspective to the incident.

The occasional confusion of tenses, however, does not seriously detract from the appeal of the paper. The narrator's voice is candid and refreshingly open. She allows the reader to share her experience. She describes small details in her surroundings, including the "faint smell of chicken livers," and the "steady drip-drip gurgle of the radiator." She relates her own physical discomfort— "I retained my cramped position, knees drawn upward, right arm underneath my breast." She uses dialogue when it is appropriate, and she shares her private responses to all that is happening.

Perhaps most important of all, she has selected a topic that is significant to her. Her final decision is important; she has committed herself physically and emotionally to a relationship. And though the last few sentences may offer an oversimplified resolution, the rest of the paper acknowledges and depicts the emotional complexities involved in her decision.

Each of the writers of the two previous papers dramatizes a specific emotional experience, but you might want to choose another writing style. You need not restrict your autobiography to the conventional writing modes of dramatization or narration; other modes might better suit your purposes. It is possible, for example, to organize your paper as a parable or extended metaphor. You might even treat your past satirically. Such an approach, however, requires you to view yourself and your life with considerable detachment. The writer of the following sketch was willing to take a long, frank, and appraising look at her life. She refers to herself in the third person and critically assesses her weaknesses.

IDA INDECISIVE

This is a story about Ida Indecisive. Ida was born in a Midwest, middle class suburb and there she has stayed her whole life. Ida has never had any problems. She grew up normally, playing with the other kids. Ida always got good grades in school. Her persuasive parents told her that that is what one must do, so she did. She continued

to get all A's and B's through high school and she still does.
Yes, Ida led a peaceful life. She never had to worry,
because she was lucky enough to have parents who would
do everything for her. I mean, she never had to decide
on anything because her persuasive parents always knew
what was the right thing to do, they knew best. Oh, it
wasn't bad, they never ordered her about or anything real
pushy. They would be very suggestive and persuasive;
Ida always thought she was the one deciding.

They would say things like, "Wouldn't you like the
pretty pink and white bicycle better than the ugly blue one?"
Of course Ida always knew the right decision. She never
had any doubt of being wrong, for if she followed all
of her parents' advice, she always came out right. After all,
she knew her parents were pretty smart.

As Ida grew older and went shopping with her mother
she again knew just what to do. If she should have to
choose between two dresses, her mother would say, "Oh,
don't you think the turquoise brings out the blue in your
eyes?" or, "Isn't the green one made better?" So again
Ida had no problem.

Ida grew older and was in high school. She joined
different clubs and groups. She always knew which ones
to join because "all her friends were." So Ida knew the
right things to do because her friends were right in there
and knew best.

Then came her true love, Denny Dominant. He was
so much fun. He always knew just what to do and how
to do it. He untaught many of the things that her persuasive
parents taught her, but Ida was seeing a new side of life
and she was having fun. Now Ida had another person to
look toward. Denny always had an answer for her. She
knew what to do if she was buying anything; she would get
blue because blue was Denny's favorite color. She always
had him to depend on.

When Ida got to be a senior in high school she had
to apply to a college. She finally had to make her own
decision. She wanted a school that nobody else in her
family had gone to. That cut out U of M and Eastern, and

State was out because it was too big. Again, her persuasive parents came through.

"Oh, you're so talented in design. Why don't you go into interior design?" Of course mother is always right. Well, that comes under home economics and Western is fairly good in that area. So that is where Ida Indecisive goes off to school. Where is Denny Dominant? Well, he made his mind up to go to a school up north so he can play basketball.

Ida has made it through one year of college. She has taken home economics and now she's not sure whether or not it's the right field. But where else could she go? Persuasive parents know that she's where she belongs. She'll come out okay. All she has to do is stick it out. Still, Ida isn't so sure. Denny Dominant knows that Ida should be with him. He understands that Ida doesn't like interior decorating. So Ida could come up north with him and be an executive secretary—that would be perfect. But Ida isn't so sure about that one either.

Since all of her life she's depended on others, Ida trusts everyone. They should know more than she does. Now Persuasive Parents and Dominant Denny have come to a complete crash. What should Ida Indecisive do? She could go north with Denny and be away from her parents, or she could stay at Western and be closer to her parents and away from Denny. Now for the first time in her life, Ida must make a decision and it's a very difficult one. She's not sure she'd like either place. She doesn't know where to turn. She's being pulled from both sides and she doesn't know which way to fall. Ida can't make the decision. She just waits and watches each day go by, hoping that some miracle will happen and take away this burden. What should she do? Which way to turn? Ida doesn't know; she has no mind of her own.

The dual perspective is especially evident in this paper. We learn about the younger girl's experience and attitude toward herself and her parents. At the same time, the tone and point of view indicate that the older narrator has gained some perception and independence. Contrary to what her last sentence suggests, her own mind is beginning to assert itself. By writing the paper she demonstrates her developing ability to independently assess her own behavior and experience.

You might also decide to design your paper as a letter. In the next example the writer modifies a letter format in a way that allows him to juxtapose his private memories with the written message. The first line of each paragraph indicates what Jim actually writes. The italicized sections indicate Jim's private reflections about the topic.

Dear Darb,
Hi, pal! Thought you'd like to hear from your old buddy.
Are you still playing football? Still the Joe Namath of
Otterbein College?

*The perfect perception, that fascinating excitement and
onmiscience of watching a rerun of a well-remembered
movie; the maples lining the field, stationary and
sweating in the grim green heat of late August. The burn
in my eyes, the salt taste. The doggedly moving forward
of my wobbly legs, cutting a weaving path through the
stillness of the summer. I still retain my adolescent
thinness, like a birch planted in the infertile dog days of
July. The presence of the coach, crew-cut and massive,
and the remembrance of the soft, pomaded admissions
counselor. The reality and the college catalogue ("Otterbein
is a place where you will grow spiritually . . . where you
will meet others . . . form lifelong friendships"). My head
aches! We started knocking heads; the hard plastic of the
Riddell helmets bounced their purple and gold sounds off the
dormitory walls overlooking the action. Everyone seemed
to want me to grind through conditioning drills or to try
to smash my face mask into my jaw. I hit! I gritted my
teeth and swallowed fear, bile, and the hope of even finding
someone I could talk to. I hit! . . . I hit! . . .*

Still in Pi Sig?

*Academically, a D in biology. 7:45. A snowy concrete path,
each student alone in his attempt to lock out the wind
and the reality of the dark, early morning. Symbiosis.
I was a clumsy, blushing Frankenstein, getting some help
in scraping off the fuzz of smalltown Ohio and adapting
to a more sophisticated part in the endless male-female
ritual. My curriculum: dealing a girl in a blurry bar, tying
a double windsor, swimming in Stroh's, throwing white
socks in the incinerator. Feedback and reinforcement while
rendering booze and stories out of my system during the
first year of my sunbathing. The Saharan concrete, the
insistent voice of WOOL. Glandular, assertive nights: the
passion-full girl from Ohio State—Holmes Hall, 754-0889—
and her demonstration of a different, particularly wet kiss.
An apt pupil.*

Going to get those pledges during Hell Week this year?

*Actives stuffing crushed ice in my pants. Made me do
exercises. (Impotence? Sterility?) Crawl. My hand slipped
on some tabasco-scented slime. A helping hand, a word,
a harried grin. Put my head over a urinespiced refrigerator
mess. I had to fill my cheeks. Crawl. Close enough to singe
my hair, then I spewed the noxious contents onto the fire.
Crawl. Sounds of deep, serious retching, a choir of
abused stomachs, still-warm vomit sticking to my hands
and knees.*

Come down to Athens—We'll show you a real party school.
How about the weekend of the seventeenth?

*Transfer. Pages of a book of many titles. Evolution. The
allusive quality of "The Waste Land." I order scotch and
soda. Don't mix wine and beer. Get rid of the short haircut.
The authority, the intellectual, the horned, prime bull.
I subscribe to* Playboy. *I get all A's and B's, and I know
how things are, and I walk the girl up a long hill in the
caressing carnival nights of April. The breath comes easily,
the smiles are natural and uncapped, and like a whore*

*who enjoys her work the smell of honeysuckle envelops us
as we cling together, tracing the stationary stars, "playing
the beast with two backs" (Othello) with my confident
artisan's skill.*

Dear Jim,
I know Darby would want me to answer . . . dead . . . dead . . .
taken from us . . . accident . . . job . . . God . . .

*   *   *

*The flab hangs heavily on my waist. I must go to the
dentist. The October leaves wave dryly in the gusts of
suddenly sharp air. I nod in grim comprehension, pull my
collar up around my bony neck, and continue descending
into the evening.*

This paper is especially skillful in communicating the growth and
development of the narrator. Jim plays a role with his friend,
Darb. His letter doesn't communicate his genuine feelings. Yet by
writing the paper and including those feelings, the narrator demonstrates that he is aware of the dichotomy between his thoughts
and his outward behavior. Jim's reflections reveal that he now
views his college experience with a different perspective. He acknowledges that his college days did not confirm his earlier
expectations. Instead of growing spiritually, he knocks heads in
football; instead of academic and intellectual achievement, he discovers fraternities, girls, liquor, and music. By the time he trans-
fers as an upperclassman he has achieved more polish and sophistication. But his vision of himself is radically altered by the news
that his friend Darb has died in an accident. Suddenly his own
mortality becomes vividly apparent. The final paragraph acknowledges evidence of his own age: gained weight and teeth in need of
repair. The implication that he has passed the prime of his life is
further emphasized by the references to October leaves waving
dryly, the gusts of suddenly sharp air, and the narrator's descent
into the evening.

Needless to say, the potential material of autobiography is
extensive. In order to give past experience a present meaning or
to impose a coherent perspective on that experience, it is often

necessary to reorder, change, or selectively omit parts of your personal experience. Obviously, the examples included in this chapter do not attempt to assess all the aspects of any writer's life. Also, some information included in the papers may be slightly altered. For instance, it is possible that the writer of "I'm Afraid There's Been a Misunderstanding" doesn't now remember exactly what the secretary looked like or the time of day she visited. She may have chosen to fill in those details from her imagination. It is not so important that the details be exactly accurate, but they should be true to the spirit and general emotional and intellectual impression the writer remembers and wishes to express. She may remember, for instance, that the interior of the office was drab but not remember the color of the desks. She may also have to invent a name and details of apparel for Mr. Stimson, whom she no longer specifically remembers. But the events, emotions, and outcomes are true to life. In some cases the setting and sequence of events are not so important as the consequences that resulted, and the writer may alter some of the material to reinforce the truth of the experience—so that the reader will best understand the nature of the experience and its meaning.

When is it reasonable to alter details? How much change is acceptable? How many details have to be changed before you no longer have autobiography but have fiction instead? These are not easy questions to answer. Writers often begin with autobiography but get so involved and intrigued with shaping their material that they end up with a piece of fiction. This topic will be treated at greater length in Chapter 9. In the final analysis, probably the only person who is qualified to determine whether a paper is primarily autobiography or primarily fiction is you, the writer, yourself. It depends on how closely you think the writing represents your life, how accurately or directly it records and expresses your experience. It also depends on what the intent of the paper is—that is, whether your central intent is self-characterization or a generalization about human experience. I am not primarily concerned here with consistently and correctly identifying writing by category—autobiography or fiction. Rather, I would like you to consider the relationship between these kinds of writing and recognize the importance of controlling your writing effectively so that your paper is expressing what you want it to express.

Autobiography is indeed challenging. Writing about oneself in the sustained, sequential, comprehensive manner I have suggested requires an honesty and insight that we often resist, for the past can yield as much pain as pleasure. Authentic autobiography involves far more than a nostalgic recollection of the past or a dreamy account of our inner life; it demands, instead, direct encounter, understanding, and evaluation. Writers of autobiography have a dual task: They need to render experience with enough dramatic immediacy to make it real; at the same time they must keep enough distance from the experience to give it an organization and clarity that will convey an understanding of the experience.

Having moved from exploration of self through encounters with place and relationships with others to autobiography, you might now continue to expand your writing experiences either toward fiction or toward nonfiction. In both cases the move is toward a wider, more varied audience (from which you are probably more distanced as a writer). These two directions are not suggested as parallel nor are they mutually exclusive endeavors. Neither is inherently more desirable than the other. Now that you have examined and expressed yourself in relation to the people, places, and things of your life, you are better prepared to write either fiction or issue-oriented papers. Your experiences and your perceptions of yourself, of places, and of people have probably provided you with raw material from which either fiction or intellectual discussions can develop and grow.

The order of the following chapters, then, is in no way intended to suggest a sequence. Since we are limited by a linear mode, we cannot discuss three topics simultaneously. If you are not interested in the issue or criticism chapters, skip to Chapter 9.

APPROPRIATE WRITING MODES

Autobiography can be written in any of the modes suggested in the previous chapter (narration or description, interview or dialogue, character sketch, dramatization). The major difference is that in autobiography, of course, the focus is not on another person, but rather on the writer's own life.

POSSIBILITIES FOR ORGANIZATION

Within the various modes you have considerable latitude in organization. The structure of a paper is in large part determined by the material and the intent of the writer. You might want to consider the following suggestions for structuring, unifying, or focusing your autobiography.

flashback

Flashback occurs when the writer interrupts the chronological flow of events with references to earlier events. There are several ways of employing flashback:

(1) Some papers are framed by present events but the body of the paper takes place in the past. Such a paper begins in the present, flashes back to an earlier period, and returns to the present at the end of the paper. For example, the writer might begin by describing a walk in the woods, flash back to an earlier walk in the woods with a loved one who is now dead, and then return at the end of the paper to the present walk in the woods.

(2) Another use of flashback is to move back and forth from past to present several times in a paper. Using this method the writer would frequently refer to the present walk in the woods while telling the story of the past event. Such an approach offers ample opportunity for a dual perspective to develop, since the reader learns directly about both the older and younger narrator.

(3) A third possibility is to give almost equal attention to past and present events, by juxtaposing memories with present activities and setting, so that the reader is learning almost simultaneously about past and present (professional example—*Portrait of the Artist as a Young Man;* student example—"I'm Afraid There's Been a Misunderstanding").

separated sections

Using this approach you might deliberately separate your paper into subdivisions, such as chapters, scenes, or acts. The division can be made on the basis of time, place, topic, and so on. The basic requirement, however, is that each section have a meaning that contributes to the meaning and intent of the paper as a whole. In other words, there should be some explicit or implicit connection between the sections that integrates the paper.

personal format

You may wish to communicate in a more personal idiom, such as a letter or diary. Many times autobiographical material is best suited to a more personal or intimate mode. One word of caution is perhaps required here: remember that you must also adjust your approach to your audience. I am not suggesting autobiography written only for yourself. The paper should be written for an audience at least as diverse as your class. You will want to modify your use of the letter or diary format accordingly. In other words, choose a diary form only if it is appropriate to the material you wish to communicate to your audience.

parable—folktale—satire—fable

These approaches stem from a much more impersonal perspective than the previous alternative. If you cast your life in the form of parable, you are required from the very start to have assessed the significance or point you wish to convey. This approach usually requires you to reduce your topic to its essentials (see "Ida Indecisive," p. 126).

repetition of imagery

You might use recurrent references to objects, memories, people, places, or activities to unify your paper. Hopefully, such recurrent images will be appropriate to the tone, intent, and central significance of the paper. At its best such imagery will contribute to the meaning of the paper also. An example of recurrent imagery can be found in "Dilemma No. 9" (see Chapter 2, p. 25), in which the writer keeps noting *Time* magazine. Her scribblings on Nixon's picture not only remind us of her physical presence in the kitchen but implicitly convey her antagonism to establishment values.

consistent focus on place, events, or relationship

The paper might be organized around a series of incidents or it might focus on a single experience. Perhaps the paper could be unified by an emphasis on place (as in "Apple Orchard," p. 75) or on a sequence of places. Another possibility is to trace the developmental stages or series of incidents contributing to a personality trait. Or you might focus on a series of encounters with one person.

exploring ideas, issues, and institutions

Although personal and immediate encounters with ourselves, our surroundings, and other people constitute a major reality in our lives, our perceptions and experiences are not limited to them. As our lives continue to develop and expand we become increasingly aware of the issues and institutions of our world. I have already mentioned Piaget's theory that we grow from the center of the self outward. Accompanying this process of decentering is the process of learning to abstract. When we are young, our lives are dominated by immediate, concrete, self-centered sensations and experiences. As we grow—becoming aware of other people and their perceptions, becoming aware of our society and other societies—we also begin to perceive the world in more abstract, more general terms.

Our generalized perceptions are, of course, strongly influenced by our personal experience. For example, your concept of marriage as a social institution has been shaped from your experience with various marriages. First you may have observed your parents' marriage; later you may have been influenced by the marriages of close relatives or friends. Television programs, books, and films (as well as magazine articles, statistical surveys, and sociological studies) have also shaped your opinions. Finally, perhaps, you have had firsthand experience in a marriage of your own. From these assorted experiences you have developed opinions and generalizations about marriage. You have also developed views and generalizations about parenthood, religion, education, friendship, war, and so on. Your relationship to issues and institutions is a reciprocal one: you are in part affected by them, and in part you shape and alter them—for people generate issues and form institutions. By exploring your involvement with issues and institutions you may learn more both about them and about yourself.

Writing about ideas, issues, and institutions requires you to move still another step beyond yourself into the world. In earlier chapters you were encouraged to focus your attention on your experiences with self, with place, and with other people. Now you must once again enlarge your vision so that you can consider an even wider variety of information and experience from which you can discuss the more abstract concerns of the world. In this chapter you are asked to extend beyond your specific personal experience, to perceive the world in a more general and abstract manner. This is not to suggest that your writing should be vague or abstract; far from it. Generalizations, proposals, or theories have little value or validity unless they are grounded in reliable, concrete evidence or particulars. You must include particulars to support your generalizations. In this respect the demands of issue-oriented writing are similar to your earlier writing experiences, for all these writings require you to provide details or evidence.

Perhaps the main difference between the writing experiences suggested in this chapter and those suggested earlier is one of emphasis. In this chapter the central emphasis is on issues or institutions rather than on the people who shape them. Certainly people are closely connected with ideas and institutions; people generate and discuss issues, and in some circumstances, people become institutions. In this sense any discussion of issues or institutions implicitly involves a discussion of people. It is likely that some of your earlier writing touched on issues or institutions, for implicit in a description of a personal experience may be a more generalized commentary on poverty, war, divorce, or urban expansion. But your primary intent in these earlier writings was to express what has happened to you, your family, and your friends. Issue-oriented writing extends beyond your immediate life. You will want to try to subordinate your own experience to the idea, issue, or institution under discussion. You may, of course, mention or refer to your own specific observations or encounters, but usually you will do so as a means of characterizing or illustrating the larger concern of the paper.

While the emphasis of the writing discussed in this chapter is on ideas, issues, and institutions, the modes and specific intent of the writing can vary widely. A paper may include some description, some narration, some argument, and some exposition, but the central thrust of an issue-oriented paper will probably be either to persuade or to inform. For example, if you wish to argue for the reform of public schools, you might narrate a specific experience you had in high school as one example of the failure of American schools to meet the needs of adolescents. You might also give a detailed description of the building itself. And you might include some statistics about the rise of high school dropouts. But all of these (narration, description, exposition) would be subordinate to your central intent, which is to argue for a reform in public education. A similar mixture of modes might occur in a paper that informs or illustrates. Keep in mind that writing is not easily classified by forms, and that any attempt to make such classifications can distort and oversimplify the organization or function of a paper. We are discussing general distinctions here, not rigid requirements.

You may write about issues and institutions in a wide range of styles. In choosing a style you will want to consider your relationship as writer to the other two elements of discourse: the topic and the audience. Let us consider each of these for a moment.

The relationship between writers and their topics varies, depending on their observation, knowledge, and experience with the topic. You may write, for instance, about an issue or institution with which you have had a good deal of firsthand observation and experience (teen-age dating customs, violence in the media, rock music as a reflection of social concerns, student protest movements, for example), or you may write about an issue with which you have had less firsthand experience (welfare reform, industrial espionage, capital punishment, and so on).

The type of support—or validation—you need is largely determined by your relationship to your topic. When you write about topics that are predominately private in character, the evidence you use—details, thoughts, examples—can be drawn largely from your own observation and experience. Such a paper has an *internal* validation. When you wish to write a paper that discusses an issue or topic in a manner that goes beyond your private experience, you often need to provide some *external* validation. If, for example, you write about your high school prom, your aging grandmother, or your childhood home, the validation—provided by descriptive details, concrete examples, or personal interpretation—can all be drawn from your own perception, memory, and beliefs. But if you want to generalize about the characteristics of adolescent dances, the problems of the aged in America, or the development of suburbs, then you have moved from a private to a public domain, and you must provide external validation for your views. In short, when you write more generally about public issues, you must make your discussion or argument publicly valid. Otherwise your audience may simply dismiss the paper as a limited, uninformed personal opinion. I am not suggesting, though, that you write impersonally. The personal dimension—important to all your writing—should be evident in the selection, interpretation, and use of evidence, as well as in the sense of commitment you bring to the topic.

You may provide external validation for your paper in several ways. For example, you can document your ideas with statistical data, historical information, scientific reports, or expert opinion. All these, however, are subject to the test of authority. Is the person or persons (the authority) who compiled or interpreted the data, the history, or the report really expert? Is your source, in other words, accurate, thorough, and reliable? There are several questions you might ask to check your sources. Is the person trained and experienced in the field you are discussing? A biochemist speaks with more authority than a sociologist about the effects of radiation on plant life; but a sociologist would speak with more authority about the history of American social customs. Another question to ask is whether the authority's opinion is relevant to the time of the events you are discussing. For example, a 1936 statistical study of high school dropouts is a valid source for a paper discussing the history of school attendance in the twentieth century, but it is not reliable as evidence of current dissatisfaction with the schools. A final question to ask as you select your external authorities is whether the source will be accepted by your audience. Some sources, though they are authoritative in the field and are up to date, are not acceptable to specific readers for other reasons. Some readers, for example, may not accept Margaret Mead's views on marriage or John Kenneth Galbraith's economic theory.

Most discussions and arguments, of course, include a mixture of both the writer's private opinion and external sources. It is not uncommon for a writer to begin a discussion of an issue by narrating or describing his or her own private encounter with that issue. Thus, you might begin a discussion of health care in American society by first talking about your grandmother or your great uncle and later citing statistics about nursing homes. In a discussion of grass-roots democracy, you might refer to your own involvement in a political movement. In some papers a good deal of the writing may be devoted to personal experience. Recall for a moment the paper discussed earlier, "On the Making of Cities" (p. 20). The writer describes and narrates how her home life was twice invaded by highway construction. The paper is both a personal history and a comment on the price we pay for urban expansion. How you mix private experience or opinion and external validation depends of course on your relationship to the topic and your purpose in writing.

You will also want to consider carefully your relationship to your audience. You may choose to write either to a small, intimate audience or to a large, public audience. As your audience increases in size and diversity and as your distance from them as a writer increases, the specific common ground you share decreases. I have already mentioned that to influence a large audience your writing must conform to conventional standards in language and organization.

As a writer you must also make other accommodations to your audience. For example, you do not want to confuse or alienate your audience by assuming that they share your personal opinions, religious beliefs, and political convictions or that their specific experiences have been similar to yours. On the other hand, you do not want to underestimate their knowledge and experience. You must be careful to avoid either omitting or misinterpreting information relevant to your topic. One way to avoid these difficulties is to establish a common ground between you and your audience—a context or a point of departure from which you can proceed. The use of standard English and common writing conventions (complete sentences, paragraphs, correct spelling and punctuation, and so on) are but a beginning. There are several ways to extend the common ground between you. One familiar means is to appeal to reason. A paper arguing for or against an issue is nearly always based on the premise that both the writer and the audience are "reasonable people." Another way to establish a common ground is to cite a recent event with which your audience is familiar and about which they will most likely share your emotional or intellectual attitudes. Still another possibility is to begin by sharing your own personal experience and then perhaps noting similar experiences you have read about. These incidents may serve as examples or simply as departure points for the discussion, analysis, or argument that follows. Finally, you might begin by presenting a variety of conflicting views about a given topic. In this way you will acknowledge the wide range of opinions held by your audience.

There are several preliminary activities that may help you collect material for writing about ideas, issues, or institutions. Once you have selected a general topic, you might write a free association on it. Give yourself a specific time limit for this, since the pressure of time keeps your mind alert. Though you probably will not want to pursue all the associations, a few of them may warrant further consideration; you could jot down explanations for some of the associations. This exercise might provide you with examples or details for your paper. It may also partially explain why you are interested in the topic.

Another possibility is to consider whether any of your experiences have influenced your views of the topic. Have you seen, heard, felt, or read anything that has affected your outlook? How does the topic touch your present life?

You might talk to several friends about the topic. Encourage them to explain their views, especially those views that differ from yours. You might also interview an assortment of people with varying opinions. Make a special effort to learn the reasons for the opinions offered. These encounters should stimulate your own thinking.

Don't worry if you haven't completely clarified your thoughts before you begin your first draft. Don't fret about the wording, sentence structure, or spelling at first. Writing the paper will help you shape your ideas. You may not discover what you really want to say until you have finished one or two drafts. Maybe you will find that you have changed your position or contradicted yourself by the end of the first draft. Perhaps you have included information that undermines your argument; maybe you have wandered off the topic. To revise the draft you might number your paragraphs and jot down in list form the main point of each paragraph. Then consider if you have explained or supported these points adequately. Check also to see if the ideas or points are arranged in a coherent pattern. This procedure should help you identify trouble spots. Maybe you have switched too abruptly from one point to another; possibly you have repeated your ideas tiresomely or included extraneous information. Most important, check to see that the paper does not sound dead, dull, and dreary. Can you "hear" your personal voice? If you are not sure how to improve the draft, ask a friend to read it aloud to you; then ask for advice.

In the following student papers, each writer approaches a topic from a different perspective, and each relies on different kinds of evidence to support that view. The writer of the first example uses neither historical fact nor written source material. Instead the information is gathered from direct observation. She establishes a common ground by sharing what she has observed.

AGE

Age isn't nice. It takes people away from other people. It prevents people from capturing their dreams. It humbles people and forces them into submission; age says you can't do the active things you've always done—you can't hack it anymore. You're getting weak, frail—you're old and the rest of your days you will spend staying alive instead of living. Age makes me sad.

My Grandfather is aged. He still has the humor and the stories he spins at the dinner table. He still has the warm gentle smile, and the big powerful frame, but I can see emptiness in his eyes. He's dying and he knows it. He can feel the power, the strength, the vitality leave his body and mind and heart every day. His shoulders droop, his skin is looser and his weight is down. He doesn't want to die but what does he have to live for? All the activities that make up his life are restricted from him; he doesn't even have complete command of his body. And most humbling of all, he needs people near him all the time in case he has a heart attack. He's not his own man anymore. He has fits of depression (unusual for his personality) quite often, and he never feels good enough to do anything. His wife is younger and healthier, and she's still living. He feels himself as a burden—a reject—unable to function properly anymore. It hurts me to see him gently caressing my dying dog and expressing his worries that she's not going to make it through the winter.

Then there's my Father. He's not as aged as Grandpa, but the years are tearing into him fast. He, like Grandpa, is 6′4″ and powerfully built. Also like Grandpa, he loves the outdoors—hunting, fishing, hiking—anything to be outside. Five years ago, Dad, through a series of very trying business problems, developed high blood pressure. Since then his strength has been leaving him like a tide in the sea— slowly, gradually at first, then gaining momentum. He can still walk twenty miles a day easily over rough terrain, but his spirit is tired. He can still go sheep and goat hunting, climbing high into the mountains and packing meat, food, etc., but he never used to say that he'd have to go slower—take it easier. And I'm not accustomed to seeing tight deep lines of worry on Mom's face when she sees him come home completely exhausted from a hunt. It scares me to realize that he should always have a hunting partner on his jaunts into the woods and mountains because—what if he didn't have enough strength to make it back, or what if he had a stroke?

Grandpa has had his last day in the field, and Dad can see his on the horizon.

Have you ever watched a person frantically trying to
complete all his dreams before time wins the race?
No. Age isn't nice at all.

Though the central intent of this paper is to inform the reader
about the consequences of old age, the bulk of the paper is descriptive. Much of the writing, in fact, could have been included in
Chapter 5. The writer vividly describes the evidence of her grandfather's and father's declining health. Yet her central purpose is
not to characterize the two men, but to emphasize how aging
affects human lives. When I mentioned earlier that the central
purpose of issue-oriented writing is usually to argue or to inform,
I also pointed out that these distinctions are often arbitrary.
"Age" is a descriptive paper that primarily informs. The paper can
also be read as a plea for greater understanding and sympathy for
old people.

The writer of the next paper also includes a good deal of
descriptive detail. In this case direct observation of a place, rather
than people, provides support for the central thesis.

I always thought that slum dwellers were lazy bums
who didn't want to escape the ghetto. Now I am at least
partially aware of some of their problems.
Last summer a couple of my friends and I were talking
about racial problems, and we realized how little contact we
had with the actual situation. We had seen a movie on the
Philadelphia ghetto, so we decided to go to New York and
walk around black Harlem to see if it was really as bad
as we had been told.
We took the train to New York and bravely boarded
a northbound subway. As soon as we stepped off the train,
the stench of rotting garbage and human waste sickened
us. It smelled as if you put a week's garbage in a closet and
opened it a month later. We almost ran up the stairs trying
to hold our breath, turning blue, rushing toward the
supposed relief of the street. A sea of heat swallowed us
as we emerged from the subway pit. The smell of decayed
garbage, of sweating shirtless bodies, of static filth
overwhelmed us on the street as well as under it.

We walked and saw bars full of silent men drinking their lunches. Mothers called their children in an English foreign to us. We saw the junkie's glazed stare. He had escaped the smell.

Though the sun shone brightly, everything was dark. The dirty heat rushed at us from the grimy sidewalk. Overflowing garbage cans on the sidewalk feasted the rats. The solid sooty wall of the unbroken row of buildings trapped the squalor. The breeze that cooled and cleaned Central Park, a few short blocks to the south, provided no relief here.

Many things about this trip impressed me, but the thing I remember most distinctly is the smell. We live in our air-conditioned suburbs and complain if the next town's factory is too smoky. We don't know what it is to always smell a filth many times worse.

Like the previous selection, this paper relies on narration and description to illustrate the thesis. The writer doesn't directly or logically argue that no one would voluntarily live in the ghetto, nor does he make vague generalizations about the deprivations of poverty. Instead he specifically describes some of the conditions of life in the slums. You may feel that the language is overly dramatic. The main characters are alternately sickened by stench, swallowed by heat, and then overwhelmed by unpleasant odors. Despite these overstatements, the writer's convictions are visibly and concretely communicated. This paper is especially interesting because the writer has incorporated writing techniques discussed in earlier chapters. His opinion is supported by a personal experience that stresses intense sensations and direct observation of a place.

It is possible, of course, to write about ghetto life, poverty, or social class from an entirely different perspective. The next writer does not describe her personal experience, but presents instead a logically organized discussion. Her thesis about "life chances" is explicitly stated in the last sentence of the opening paragraph. The paragraphs that follow present and amplify evidence supporting that thesis. Because she is more removed from her topic, the writer relies heavily on external validation.

LIFE CHANCES[1]

Born of middle class status, I never stopped to think
about just how lucky I was. Money to me did not seem very
important, but then we never suffered from the lack of it.
Then I realized that I always had proper medical care,
food to eat, a good education, and many other comforts
of life. These things were going to make my life chances
favorable, because the key to the best life chances is wealth.

Life chances are those things in life which don't
directly have price tags yet are influenced greatly by what
one can afford. They include such things as life expectancy,
infant mortality rate, possibility of accident, and health
standards. One's life chances are the probabilities that an
individual will attain or fail to attain important goals and
experiences in life.

Statistics show that social class has a high correlation
with the life chances, and wealth has a significant effect
on social-class standing. If a child begins with such a lack
of wealth as to make it impossible for him, even with all
his efforts combined, to jump up and reach the lowest
rung of the ladder to success, there is no way he can attempt
and ascent to the top or even just to the next rung. The
lower-class people are trapped in their poor life style from
the day they are born. Their lack of money will influence
their life chances greatly.

Social class has also been shown to have a high
correlation with mortality rates. The most reliable
comparisons are those between whites, who can be
designated as the higher-status group, and blacks, with a
lower social status. The Census Bureau estimates that a
newborn white male can expect to live to be 67½ years old,
whereas his black counterpart will have a life expectancy
of only 61 years. There are similar discrepancies
between white and black female children. The mortality
rate for female white babies in the first year of their lives

[1] Footnotes have been omitted from this paper.

is 1.6 percent. For black female babies, the rate is twice as high, 3.2 percent. The chance that the baby's mother will die in childbirth is four times as great if she is Negro than if she is white.

Other statistics bring up the class-linked health problems of the low-status American. There is an increased incidence of heart disease, diabetes, and tuberculosis among the poor. The incidence of new active cases of tuberculosis among Indians is seven times the national average. Malnutrition is also common among the poor. As stated by George McGovern in his report *The Food Gap,* "There are an estimated thirty-seven million Americans with incomes too low to provide themselves with a nutritionally correct diet." Malnutrition in expectant mothers is highly correlated with premature and stillbirths and can cause permanent brain damage and stunted physical and mental development in their offspring. The United States Public Health Service says that one out of every three children in poor families in the U.S. is so anemic that he should have immediate medical attention. Some industrially caused diseases, such as black lung and cancer produced by asbestos particles, are found only among those unskilled workers of low status who must work in such health-hazardous industries. Low-status people not only fall ill more often, but they also can afford to purchase less in the way of medical attention. For example, a survey in California by Morris Axelord, a leading sociologist, showed that Mexican-Americans made 2.3 visits to a doctor per year, compared with 5.6 for other residents of the state.

In addition to illness, low-status Americans have more accidents. Household accidents, such as carbon monoxide poisoning often caused by space heaters that are needed to keep substandard dwellings warm in the wintertime, lead poisoning from flaking paint, fires, and falls, occur much more frequently in lower-class homes. The victims of industrial accidents also come almost entirely from the lower classes. With all these hazards surrounding the lower class, one can easily see that it would be very difficult for them to break away from their low status.

Through experiences in my own life, and statistics
I've cited above, it seems quite evident that social status
influenced by the amount of money one has greatly
affects one's life chances. The lower-status people will
most likely never have the chances to enjoy the comforts
of a healthy life which I have enjoyed. Thus trapped in
their vicious life cycles, the poor will remain poor, while
the rich remain rich.

The author's relationship to her topic is clearly established in the
opening paragraph. Her middle-class background has insulated her
from the problems faced by families of lower socio-economic
levels. The organization and tone of the paper differ considerably
from the first two selections. Though the writer of "Life Chances"
begins and ends her paper on an explicitly personal note, she
deliberately removes herself from the main section of the paper.
She does not try to persuade us by the force of her feelings or by
dramatizing a personal experience. Instead she lets the examples
and statistics speak for her. The tone of the paper is more infor-
mational than persuasive.

Perhaps the most serious weakness in this paper is its failure
to distinguish clearly the relationship between social class, race,
financial status, and occupation. There is a statistical relationship
between these, but the writer attempts to make a causal relationship also. She links money to social class and social class to race.
Money may partially determine social class, but social class does
not determine race. The writer might consider either clarifying or
omitting the discussion of causality.

The three examples we have discussed so far in this chapter
differ in purpose, tone, and organization. In each paper the writer
establishes a different relationship with the topic and the audience.
Of the three, the author of "Life Chances" is most distant from
her topic. She acknowledges that she has had no direct experience
with poverty. She includes numerous external sources and she
adopts a language and tone suitable for addressing a wide audience. The writer of the second selection is closer to his topic. He
has toured Harlem and observed living conditions there. His tone
is informal. He doesn't argue his point directly. The first writer is
closest to her topic. Though she herself is not old, she is living

daily with people who are aging. She is directly affected by what she sees; she states her thesis explicitly and her emotions openly. By doing so she establishes a more intimate relationship with her audience.

When you write about issues or institutions, you need not be as serious as the previous writers. You may adopt a humorous or ironic tone if you wish. You might even write a parody or fable to communicate your opinion. In the next example Clare Boothe Luce parodies Hamlet's famous soliloquy. Her topic is Watergate and her point is a serious one, despite the surface humor.

A SOLILOQUY[2]

To impeach, or not to impeach: that is the question.
Whether 'tis better for the Party to suffer
The slings and arrows of outrageous Nixon,
Or now to drown him in his sea of troubles,
And by voting, end him. Impeach; convict;
No more; and by convicting say we ended
Watergate, restored the public trust,
Upheld the Constitution, purified
Our politics, and got Sam Ervin off
Of Television. 'Tis a consummation
Devoutedly to be wished. Impeach. Convict.
Convict: Perchance acquit! Ay, there's the rub:
For in that long and bitter process
Of impeachment, what evils may befall us
While we are shuffling off his White House coil
Must give us pause: To deepen those divisions
Now dividing us the more, to down
Dow Jones to Davy's locker deeper, drive
Bankrupted brokers to despairful leaps
From Wall Street's darkened windows, stoke the fires
Of wild inflation, court depression,
And be left ourselves to ration gasoline!
Impeach: Whilst wav'ring allies, heeding not

Th'unmastered Henry, yield to Cairo's will
And Moscow slyly strokes the Arab hand
That holds the bung of Sheikdom's oily drums.
And whispers in the vengeful Moslem ear,
The plotted Diaspora of the Jews.
Impeach: To strike the sword from his command—
That U.S. sword he only holds to guard
Our skies and shores from Russian infestation—
And in this hour of the sheathéd sword
And unhailed Chief, to court atomic doom!
For who would bear the whips and scorns of Nixon's
Insolence in office, his oppressive vetoes,
His scrambled tapes, his plumbers, his Bebe,
His vaunted innocence, the law's delay,
The exile of the Court of Camelot
And noble Galbraith, Reston, Schlesinger,
The pangs of unrequited Liberalism,
The long-drawn martyrdom of Alger Hiss,
When we ourselves might Dick's quietus make
With bold impeachment? Ay, what Party
With e'en a tarnished Kennedy in hand
Would grunt and sweat out three more years of Dick
But that the dread of pitfalls on the road
To his conviction puzzles still the will,
And makes us rather bear the ills we have
Than fly to others that we know not of?
Thus conscience doth make cowards of us all,
And thus our native hue of partisanship,
Is sicklied o'er by the pale cast of patriotism,
And politics of great pitch and moment.
With these regards their currents turn awry,
And lose the name of action. Soft you now!
The fair Kay Graham! Nymph, in the columns, please
Be all our fears remembered.

Several comments on the events and consequences of Watergate
are evident in this parody. The writer directs her humor at the
television hearings, financial concerns, and international relations.
She also refers to several political figures who were somehow in-

volved in the turmoil. The use of Hamlet's speech as a structure for the parody is especially appropriate, since it implicitly compares Hamlet's indecision to the inability of Americans to take decisive action on Watergate.

The next two essays focus on the role of women. The first was published in *Ms* magazine and the second in *Reader's Digest*. The two writers differ distinctly in their views and writing styles. The first writer adopts a semi-serious, semi-ironic tone. She begins by relating a brief encounter with a friend and then proceeds in declamatory style to catalogue and berate the traditional responsibilities of a wife. The writer of the second essay is also a woman. In a relaxed, informal, but genuine tone she advocates the very behavior mocked by the first writer. The essays are reprinted here with minimal introduction and no concluding commentary. The personal voices of the writers are obvious. See if you can distinguish the characteristics of each woman's voice and her method of organization. Can you imagine either writer adopting the other's style? How does each establish her relationship to the reader? After discussing the essays in class you might want to write your own opinion on the issue of male or female roles.

WHY I WANT A WIFE[3]

I belong to that classification of people known as wives. I am A Wife. And, not altogether incidentally, I am a mother.

Not too long ago a male friend of mine appeared on the scene fresh from a recent divorce. He had one child, who is, of course, with his ex-wife. He is obviously looking for another wife. As I thought about him while I was ironing one evening, it suddenly occurred to me that I, too, would like to have a wife? Why do I want a wife?

I would like to go back to school so that I can become economically independent, support myself, and, if need be, support those dependent upon me. I want a wife who will work and send me to school. And while I am going to school

I want a wife to take care of my children. I want a wife to keep track of the children's doctor and dentist appointments. And to keep track of mine, too. I want a wife to make sure my children eat properly and are kept clean. I want a wife who will wash the children's clothes and keep them mended. I want a wife who is a good nurturant attendant to my children, who arranges for their schooling, makes sure that they have an adequate social life with their peers, takes them to the park, the zoo, etc. I want a wife who takes care of the children when they are sick, a wife who arranges to be around when the children need special care, because, of course, I cannot miss classes at school. My wife must arrange to lose time at work and not lose the job. It may mean a small cut in my wife's income from time to time, but I guess I can tolerate that. Needless to say, my wife will arrange and pay for the care of the children while my wife is working.

I want a wife who will take care of *my* physical needs. I want a wife who will keep my house clean. A wife who will pick up after me. I want a wife who will keep my clothes clean, ironed, mended, replaced when need be, and who will see to it that my personal things are kept in their proper place so that I can find what I need the minute I need it. I want a wife who cooks the meals, a wife who is a *good* cook. I want a wife who will plan the menus, do the necessary grocery shopping, prepare the meals, serve them pleasantly, and then do the cleaning up while I do my studying. I want a wife who will care for me when I am sick and sympathize with my pain and loss of time from school. I want a wife to go along when our family takes a vacation so that someone can continue to care for me and my children when I need a rest and change of scene.

I want a wife who will not bother me with rambling complaints about a wife's duties. But I want a wife who will listen to me when I feel the need to explain a rather difficult point I have come across in my course of studies. And I want a wife who will type my papers for me when I have written them.

I want a wife who will take care of the details of my social life. When my wife and I are invited out by my friends, I want a wife who will take care of the babysitting arrangements. When I meet people at school that I like and want to entertain, I want a wife who will have the house clean, will prepare a special meal, serve it to me and my friends, and not interrupt when I talk about the things that interest me and my friends. I want a wife who will have arranged that the children are fed and ready for bed before the guests arrive so that the children do not bother us. I want a wife who takes care of the needs of my guests so that they feel comfortable, who makes sure that they have an astray, that they are passed the hors d'oeuvres, that they are offered a second helping of the food, that their wine glasses are replenished when necessary, that their coffee is served to them as they like it. And I want a wife who knows that sometimes I need a night out by myself.

I want a wife who is sensitive to my sexual needs, a wife who makes love passionately and eagerly when I feel like it, a wife who makes sure that I am satisfied. And, of course, I want a wife who will not demand sexual attention when I am not in the mood for it. I want a wife who assumes the complete responsibility for birth control, because I do not want more children. I want a wife who will remain sexually faithful to me so that I do not have to clutter up my intellectual life with jealousies. And I want a wife who understands that *my* sexual needs may entail more than strict adherence to monogamy. I must, after all, be able to relate to people as fully as possible.

If, by chance, I find another person more suitable as a wife than the wife I already have, I want the liberty to replace my present wife with another one. Naturally, I will expect a fresh, new life; my wife will take the children and be solely responsible for them so that I am left free.

When I am through with school and have a job, I want my wife to quit working and remain at home so that my wife can more fully and completely take care of a wife's duties.

My God, who *wouldn't* want a wife?

THE ADVENTURE OF BEING A WIFE[4]

As a minister's wife, I'm asked to speak occasionally
to church groups and women's clubs. Quite often, when
I do, a woman will come up to me afterward and bewail
the monotony of her life. She feels trapped, she's frustrated,
her talents are withering on the vine. But what, she adds
with a despairing shrug, can she do? After all, she's only
a wife.

Only a wife! At times I feel like taking the woman by
the shoulders and shaking her. Here you are, I want to say,
caught up in the most marvelous adventure a woman can
experience, and you don't know it!

Thirty-six years of being a wife have utterly convinced
me that no job, no hobby, no activity on earth can compare
with the drama and exhilaration of living with a man,
loving him, doing your best to understand his infinitely
complex mechanism and helping to make it hum and sing
and soar the way it was designed to do.

Is this easy? Of course not! It takes skill and
selflessness. You have to use your heart and your head.
But it can be done, and when it is—well, what *is* adventure?
It's the discovery of new powers and new dimensions, the
opportunity for self-testing, the happiness that comes
from high achievement. These are the promises hidden in
every marriage—if only a woman will reach out and
claim them.

If I were invited into a young wife's kitchen to have
a cup of coffee and talk about what she might do to make
and keep her marriage exciting, here are some of the
suggestions I would make.

Study your man, as if he were a strange and rare
and fascinating animal—which indeed he is! Study him
ceaselessly, because he will be constantly changing. Take
pride in his strengths and achievements, but analyze his
areas of weakness, too. Before my two daughters were

married, I told them: "You have fallen in love. You're dazzled by a man's brilliance, his confidence, his charm. You have yet to encounter his uncertainties and inadequacies. But this is where you can *really* love him, *really* help him, *really* be a wife. So don't be dismayed or disillusioned when you discover these aspects of him."

Respect his work. When you marry a man, you also marry his job. At times you may even feel that the job comes before you. It doesn't, really, but doing his work well means as much to a man as motherhood does to a woman—and for much the same reasons.

Learn the tricky and challenging art of absorption. A lot of unsuccessful wives seem to regard themselves as divinely appointed receiving stations for love. They're constantly concerned with how much attention and affection they're getting. Certainly a wife is entitled to love and loyalty. But she also has to be ready to absorb irritability on the part of her husband at times, flashes of displaced anger, discontent with his own performance. These things have to find an outlet somewhere. If a wife can think of herself as a kind of lightning rod that conducts fear and frustration harmlessly into the ground, not only will she be of inestimable value to her husband but she will grow tremendously as a person herself.

And remember: Even when a man becomes successful, and knows it, some hidden, sensitive, unsure part of him continues to need the unquestioning support and loyalty of a loving woman. Perhaps it's a remnant in him of the little boy who once turned to his mother for reassurance. Whatever it is, it's there.

Practice the art of listening. Most men desperately need a sounding board against which to test ideas, hopes, dreams, ambitions, problems, inner conflicts that they can't resolve alone. They need a feminine listener, one to whom then can confide their innermost thoughts and feelings without fear of ridicule or rejection.

Creative listening involves response, communication, exchange of ideas. But there are also times when a wife has to be silent, has to bite her tongue, hold back the sharp word that will turn an argument into a fight, or a bad situation into a worse one. No doubt her husband has an equal responsibility. But I think that a man's job, basically, is to tame the world; a wife's job is to control herself— and indirectly her husband.

Let him know that you need him. Not long ago an outraged young wife told me that she was fed up with her husband's roving eye. She was going to tell him off, divorce him if he so much as looked at another woman. I said to her, "Do you really want a solution to all this? Then go to your husband. Ask him to put his arms around you. When he does, say to him, 'Darling, I'm hurt. I'm unhappy, and I think you know why. I'm your wife. Please hold me. Please help me.' That's all you have to do. The admission of your need of his love will work miracles where no amount of anger can. Try it; you will see."

Use your talents. Marriage need not limit your horizons. If you have a gift for design, or photography, or decorating, or writing poetry—any talent at all—don't let it gather dust; use it to expand your marriage.

A brilliant girl I know, who graduated *magna cum laude* and went on to graduate work, now has three small children and all the attendant household chores. "I need every single thing I learned in college," she maintains, "to understand my husband's business, to run his home efficiently and to keep myself aware of what's going on in the world."

There are so many little common-sense don'ts that help a wife to make marriage an adventure. For example, don't make an issue over small things. Overlook them and you will find that your opinion carries a lot more weight in big things!

Don't be afraid to compromise—compromise doesn't mean giving in. It's simply an adult way of acknowledging that there are points of view other than your own in this complex world, and realizing that some of them occasionally may be right.

Don't be alarmed if you and your husband differ about some things. Marriage is a partnership, not a merger of identities. One of the happiest women I know, a rock-ribbed Republican, has a husband who gave up a lucrative job to work for the Democratic administration. "No problem," she says cheerfully. "I married a man, not a set of political beliefs." And he accepts their differences just as calmly.

Don't keep fretting over irretrievable mistakes. Everybody makes them. The best thing to do is learn from them and then forget them. I must say, some women seem to be incapable of this—especially if their husbands are guilty of the errors.

There are many small common-sense dos as well as don'ts. Expand and develop the art of sharing—not just the big, serious things, but the little, delightful things: the book you're reading, the joke that you heard and hoard for him, the sunset you call him to watch, the entrancing, unbelievable thing your three-year-old said. Even shared exasperation can be fun!

Perhaps the simplest and most inclusive of all rules for successful wives is this: try to please your husband. Does he like neatness? You can be neat. Does he like friends around him? Learn to entertain. Is his job a stressful one? Make his home an oasis of quietness in a noisy world. Does he want you around? Thank heaven—and be available. This kind of concern is an expression of love, and it's impossible to give it without having it reflected back to you.

"To love and to cherish, till death do us part. . . ." This is the great, soul-satisfying role of a wife. And never make the mistake of thinking it a secondary role. Where the ship of matrimony is concerned, your husband may be the motor, but you're the rudder—and it's the rudder that determines where the ship will go!

In a very real sense, writing an issue-oriented paper is a challenging and complex process. As a curious, inquiring writer, you gather private and public information relevant to the topic. You also must consider, analyze, interpret, draw conclusions about, or evaluate that information. Once you have clarified your position, you must then organize a paper that clearly communicates and supports that position. The organization should reflect the perspective and conclusion reached after you have observed, recalled, read, considered, and evaluated all the relevant material.

It is misleading, however, to assume that writers know exactly what they will say before they begin to write. Though some thought and discussion usually precede writing, the very process of writing itself will help clarify your thinking. For example, when you compose that first draft of your paper, you may find that you have unconsciously shifted your position by the end of the paper. This is not uncommon, for as you write you will be forced to examine closely how you interpret and evaluate information. By writing down your responses to an issue and your critical assessment of relevant information, you may in fact alter your original opinion or shift the emphasis of the paper. When this happens, you must then revise the paper in light of your new perceptions so that the ideas are presented coherently and consistently. Early drafts may be inconsistent or disorganized, for in these "working papers" you are seeking to establish the purpose, tone, organization—the style of the paper. Once these matters are settled in your own mind and in your rough drafts, you can write a more polished paper controlled by an informed, consistent, authoritative voice. Your control and authority, as well as the tone of the paper, will be apparent from the very first paragraph.

SPECIFIC WRITING POSSIBILITIES

Visit a local institution (school, nursing home, city council, for example) and write a paper about it.

Write a parody, fable, or parable about some aspect of life on campus.

Write a humorous essay that points out foibles or inconsistencies in our society.

Select a topic about which you have changed your views and write a paper that explains when and why you changed your mind.

Write a dialogue in which two hypothetical opponents are discussing an issue.

Talk to several friends who have different views on an issue, idea, or institution. Write a paper that discusses the different opinions and includes your own opinion.

Select a controversial topic and argue for it or against it in two or three different styles. Experiment by shifting the tone, the method of organization, or the distance between you and the reader.

Make a list of the five issues that you feel are the most critical issues of the twentieth century. Write a paper which discusses how one of these touches or influences your life.

Select a news article or editorial with which you disagree and write an answer to it.

toward criticism

I began the previous chapter by pointing out that writing about issues and institutions requires you to view the world in abstract terms—to generalize from your perceptions and experiences. Critical writing also requires you to stretch beyond your immediate encounters with self, place, and others. Broadly speaking, the central function of critical writing is to offer an evaluation or judgment of a work or phenomenon.

As a critic you will be discovering and clarifying the abstract values and standards that guide your evaluations. Most of these values have their roots in your prior experience. Your opinions about art, morality, and social responsibility, for example, are shaped by what you have seen, felt, heard, or read. In a very real sense, critical writing is a natural extension of the earlier writing you have done for this class. As a critic you will be continuing to discover, explore, and shape yourself. You will be discovering the sources and exploring the reasons for your judgments. At the same time you will be extending yourself beyond your immediate sensations and encounters with self, place, and others. When you criticize, you are developing your tastes, generalizing your views, and clarifying the principles that structure your opinions. Finally, you are using those principles and generalizations to make judgments about the world.

You have probably had considerable critical experience already. Learning to evaluate or appraise has been a natural part of your development as a human being. You make many judgments in your everyday life. Most are routine, but others can have decisively significant consequences. You judge the quality of food, the reliability of the media, and the dependability of your friends; you may also devote some time to self-evaluation. When you make these appraisals, you are functioning as a critic.

In some ways you have already been acting as a critic in this class. Some of your earlier writings undoubtedly reflect your critical tastes. You are also functioning as a critic when you respond to your classmates' papers. In a significant sense, this chapter on criticism repeats and extends observations and advice offered earlier in this book. Chapter 2 was intended to help you develop your critical skills. In fact, it might be helpful for you to reread that chapter before you begin to write a critical paper.

Criticism can be highly specialized and sophisticated writing undertaken by an expert who is technically knowledgeable and culturally experienced with the subject. In this chapter, however, I do not wish to define criticism so narrowly. Rather we will be considering criticism in a broader sense, which includes informed, personal responses and explanations, as well as analysis, interpretation, and evaluation. This is not to say that you can be lax in providing adequate evidence or in clearly demonstrating the basis of your critical views. I want you to offer your considered, organized, and supported opinion, but I do not expect you to become professional critics. My purpose is to introduce you to the skills, practices, and procedures that are helpful to a critic. Remember too that criticism need not be regarded as a pejorative term. I am speaking of the critic as one who responds to the merits as well as the shortcomings of a subject.

Your choice of topic as a critical writer is nearly unlimited. You may focus on works of art, institutions, movements, customs, sports events, or other phenomena. Your range of topics is even greater than it was in the previous chapter. It is important, of course, for you to select a topic that interests you. You might choose an annoying television program, an engrossing film, a puzzling short story, or a stimulating rock concert. You do not have to select a specific work or event, however. You could discuss recent trends in country music, in fashion, or in children's literature, for example.

Once you have selected your topic, there are several ways you can begin. The following suggestions are offered only as possible ways to proceed. You may decide to develop your own methods for writing a critical paper.

Let's assume that you want to write a paper on a recent film. Films offer a special challenge, for unlike printed material they are not easily reexamined. You will want to make a special effort to keep track of your responses. If possible, plan to see the film more than once.

After seeing the film, you might jot down in a list or in brief paragraphs your immediate positive and negative responses. What did you like and what did you dislike? You might also summarize the plot or sequence of events in the film. Next, record any questions you have about what happened in the film or why it happened. Consider anything that seems to be inconsistent, out of order, or somehow distracting from the central development of the film. Finally, you might list any other films that you could compare or contrast to this one.

When you have recorded your immediate responses, you might consider the possible sources and reasons for those responses. Give some thought to *why* you liked or disliked parts of the film. If you were dissatisfied with the end of the movie, for example, list possible reasons for your dissatisfaction. Perhaps the ending was inconsistent with the rest of the events or inconsistent with your own experience. Perhaps you were dissatisfied with the social implications of the ending. Next, you might go back to your list of questions and consider possible explanations for them. Even if you are not sure of these answers, record them briefly for later reference.

You might also review your outline or plot summary. Can you detect any overall pattern or design to the film? Is there any pattern to the events, the behavior of characters, or the use of setting? If you discern any patterns, you might sketch them in a graph or summarize them briefly.

Before you begin to write a draft of your paper, you may want to discuss the film with some friends. What are their opinions? How do they respond to your comments? Do they have any answers to your questions about the film? Don't talk only to people who agree with you; make a special effort to find someone who disagrees. Talking about your ideas will undoubtedly help you to clarify and organize them.

Finally, if you wish, you can read some secondary sources—perhaps a professional review of the film. If you know something about the history of film or about camera techniques, you should consider the film in light of that knowledge. If you are a novice at film criticism, you might want to read some books about the structure of film. These last steps are not always necessary or desirable, but sometimes they are helpful.

As you talk to others and formulate your own judgments of film, television, books, or other works, you will be discovering, exploring, and shaping your own value systems. Your judgment or assessment of a work derives from the critical standards you bring to the film. You may not be immediately aware of the sources, reasons, or criteria that foster your responses, but thoughtful attention may enable you to discover and clarify the values influencing your judgments.

Critical opinions are usually guided by aesthetic (having to do with beauty or taste), moral (having to do with right or wrong), psychological, historical, or social perspectives. It is not always possible or even desirable to separate your opinions according to these categories. Many of your views, in fact, are not clearly delimited according to these classifications, but are a blend of more than one. The distinctions, when they can be made, are usually a matter of emphasis. Considering your ideas according to these categories can be helpful, however, for purposes of organizing and clarifying your writing.

Let's consider each of these critical perspectives in the context of the hypothetical film we have been discussing. You may not be aware of them, but some kind of standards are implicit in your assessment of the film. For example, if you faulted the film for misrepresenting the welfare situation in America, you would be judging the film from a social perspective. If you praised the film for realistically portraying the emotional deterioration of the central character, your judgment is largely psychological. If you object to unnecessary (or unjustified) scenes of violence, you are bringing both aesthetic and moral standards to bear on the film. By praising a film for its technical inventiveness, you may be assessing it both from an aesthetic perspective (the internal consistency) and a historical view (how it differs from previous films).

These perspectives can be brought to bear on any topic. You might criticize a novel from an artistic, or aesthetic, perspective that emphasizes the unity of the work, the characterization, or the patterns of imagery. This approach might be especially suitable for a literary audience. You might also discuss it from a historical perspective—its place in respect to previous novels dealing with the same theme or written in the same period. Or perhaps you would like to criticize the social or moral implications of the novel—how it reflects contemporary social values. If your topic is popular music, you might judge some songs as being either morally offensive or socially relevant. Whatever your topic, you will want to discover and clarify the standards guiding your opinions.

You may not discover or clarify your critical perspective until you begin to organize and express your opinion in a rough draft. As you become more aware of your critical standards, however, you will want to clarify them for your readers. You may, in fact, wish to explain your standards within the essay itself (depending on your audience). There is no need, for example, to explain standards of good poetry to your English instructor, but you may have to explain to that same instructor the criteria by which you judge the latest racing cars. If your audience is unfamiliar with the topic (whether it be music or racing cars) and the criteria applicable to the topic, you must make those standards clear in your essay. If you are writing to an audience familiar with rock music or racing cars, the explicit statement of standards is not as necessary.

The examples and details you select to support your critical view will depend on your criteria. Your paper should clearly illustrate how a work either does or does not meet your standards. If you are proposing that *A Separate Peace* is a well-unified novel, you will want to point out the structural or thematic devices that contribute to its unity. If you maintain that a current television family comedy is trite and repetitious, you will want to cite recurrent patterns in specific episodes or cite mundane, overused comic techniques in the series. If you are discussing suspension bridges as a significant advance in architectural design, you will want to explain how these bridges are both different from and superior to previous bridges. And, of course (as in your previous writing), you will want to select examples and details that are both accurate and reliable.

I have already emphasized that critical papers are written in a wide variety of writing styles—ranging from the personal, familiar style to a more formal, distant style. As always, your choice of style will depend on your relationship to your reader and to your topic. You might, for example, communicate your critical opinion of rock music in the fifties to a small group of your friends who are well versed in rock music. You might, on the other hand, interpret the meaning of an eighteenth-century political movement for an audience that is unfamiliar with eighteenth-century history. Or finally, you might publicly evaluate the significance of violence in the media for a large, diverse audience. As in your previous writing experiences, the language, tone, and examples you use in a critical essay will depend on your distance from your audience and from your topic.

The following introductory statements were taken from commentaries on the meaning of the deaths of Janis Joplin and Jimi Hendrix. The first two were published in the *New York Times* and the third was published in *Life*. Notice that each writer immediately establishes his relationship to his topic and his audience.

JANIS JOPLIN 1943–1970[1]

God, what a year this is turning out to be. As if the mass violence at Kent State weren't enough, we now seem to be caught in an almost hypnotic string of personal violence. Three weeks ago, Jimi Hendrix, and now Janis Joplin. The king and the queen of the gloriously self-expressive music that came surging out of the late sixties are dead, the victims, directly or indirectly, of the very real physical excesses that were part of the world that surrounded them.

[1] Don Heckman, *New York Times,* 11 October 1970, Sec. II, p. 29.

OVERDOSING ON LIFE[2]

Most likely, neither Jimi Hendrix nor Janis Joplin meant much of anything to you. Jimi died on September 18th, Janis on October 4th, both, it was said, in connection with drugs. They were young rock stars. A little over three years ago, only the most ardent music buffs had heard of either of them.

Perhaps you generally keep abreast, yet never heard of Jimi alive—nor of Janis for that matter. Perhaps you read of them for the first time in this newspaper—struck, fleetingly, tsk, at the coincidence: "Second this month, isn't it?" perhaps right where you're reading this now: an office, a coffee shop, a commuter train. Forgive me, I am trying to get a picture of you. Asked to comment on their deaths for this page, I feel like a kind of foreign correspondent.

DRUGS AND DEATH
IN THE RUN-DOWN WORLD OF ROCK MUSIC[3]

First, it was Jimi Hendrix, rock's flamboyant super star, snuffed out last month at 27, dead on arrival at a London hospital. The cause? Suffocation from vomiting while unconscious from sleeping pills. Accidental overdose? Suicide? The coroner could not say.

Then it was Janis Joplin, rock's greatest soul belter, also 27, found dead on the floor of a Los Angeles motel room last week, fresh needle marks on her left arm, a red balloon filled with a white powder stashed in her trash can. Coroner's finding: overdose of drugs.

The writer of the first selection is obviously moved by the two deaths. His opening sentence, which is directed toward an understanding and sympathetic audience, establishes his emotional response. By associating the deaths of the rock stars with the Kent State killings, he also establishes a political and social context from which we can view all three events.

The writer of the second selection directs his comments to

[2] Jacob Brackman, *New York Times,* 27 October 1970, p. 45.
[3] Albert Goldman, *Life,* 16 October 1970, pp. 32–33.

readers who are more distant and detached from the rock scene. He is talking to middle-aged America, and despite the partially submerged irony of his tone, he is clearly trying to bridge the gap between his own perspective and that of his audience. Because he assumes his readers know little of either star, his essay probably will differ considerably from the first one. He may have to introduce information that would be common knowledge to another audience.

The writer of the third selection is the most detached from his topic and his audience. He states the facts without emotion. The two staccato statements about the coroner's reports and the matter-of-fact descriptions of the circumstances of each death emphasize the analytic perspective he brings to the topic. The excerpt reads much like a post-mortem report.

None of these excerpts is long enough for us to discern the critical perspective of the entire essay. It is clear, however, that each writer's relation to his audience and topic will influence the tone, design, and choice of examples in each essay.

I said earlier that I was defining criticism in broad terms. You may experiment with several critical approaches, ranging from a brief informal review to a more detailed analysis or interpretation. You can find examples of informal reviews in weekly news magazines or your local newspaper. Below are two reviews of *The Sting.* The first was written by a student for a campus paper several months after the film was released; the second was written by a professional critic for *Time,* shortly after the film was released.

The Sting brings what may be the best male acting team of the '60's and '70's back together again. Robert Redford and Paul Newman head a cast that walked away with everything but the kitchen sink in this year's Academy Awards, winning seven Oscars, including Best Picture. The main tune from *The Sting* called "The Entertainer" is also a hit. Add this all together and the total is an excellent movie.

The story revolves around two con men of 1939 in Chicago who are out to put "the sting" to a racketeer who had another con man killed. Robert Redford plays Johnny Hooker, who is a drifter, a con man that moves from town to town playing small confidence games. Paul Newman portrays Harry Gonfarb, a pro that plays the "big street," the rich in the big cities like New York and Chicago.

Action takes place as "the sting" is being set up, executed and completed. Minor problems such as a police detective from Joliet, Ill. chasing Redford for giving him counterfeit money in a payoff and the FBI chasing Newman for a stock swindle have to be worked around to complete the sting. And this doesn't count the mob trying to kill Redford for stealing money from them.

There are plenty of twists to this plot, coupled with good performances from the whole cast. Add to this a surprise ending and you have an evening's worth of entertainment. *The Sting* is well worth seeing once, and a second time to enjoy the action you missed the first time around.[4]

CON GAME[5]

This isn't a movie, it's a recipe. The people who put *The Sting* together followed the instructions on the *Butch Cassidy* package: one Paul Newman, one Robert Redford, a dash of caper. Stir in the same director, if available.

He was. *Butch Cassidy* may not have been very good, but it made a bundle, so what difference does it make? Newman and Redford pass a few facial expressions between them and try to cool each other out. If there ever was much of a script, it can be said to have gone to waste.

The movie, set in Chicago and environs during the '30s, concerns a sophomore con man (Redford), a grizzled veteran con man (Newman) and their extravagant scheme to bilk a big-money hoodlum from New York (Robert Shaw). There is a tangle of subplots, some slothful suspense and an ending of telegraphed surprise.

The Sting was not made to be taken seriously, but many people find it difficult to enjoy the movie casually. It lacks the elements that could have given it true drive: a sense

---

[4] *The Statesman* (California State College, Bakersfield), June 1974, p. 4.
[5] Jay Cocks, *Time,* 31 December 1973, pp. 50–51. Reprinted by permission from *Time,* The Weekly Newsmagazine; Copyright Time Inc.

of an urban underworld, or of the Depression that sucked so many people into it; understanding of the con man's pathology that goes beyond surface style and patter; a story that depends not on plot twists but on characters. The movie ends up with a lot of expensive sets and a screenful of blue eyes.

Clearly these writers differ not only in opinion but in writing style. The first writer devotes most of his review to a plot summary. His evaluative statements are restricted to a few scattered phrases such as "excellent movie," "good performances" and "well worth seeing." He doesn't explain why the film is excellent except to say that it won several awards and is entertaining. The review serves mainly as a descriptive commentary.

The second reviewer devotes only one brief paragraph to a plot summary. The rest of his comments are evaluative, drawn primarily from an aesthetic perspective. In the opening metaphor, he faults the film for being derivative of *Butch Cassidy*. He goes on to attack the superficial acting, the weak script, the "slothful" suspense and the lack of depth in characterization. He does not, however, offer many examples or details to support his judgment.

The next example, which was published in a campus newspaper, reviews a rock album. The writer discusses The Band from aesthetic and historical perspectives. He traces the development of The Band from their association with Bob Dylan to their most recent album, "Rock of Ages."

ROCK OF AGES[6]

Bob Dylan should never have made it. When he was releasing his avant-garde songs back in the sixties, people explained them as the result of a warp in the records—or in his mind. It was all just too much more than people were asking for.

Paradoxically, however, many of Dylan's songs became well known classics. Singers who wanted to be considered "in" always had some Dylan in their repertoires. The names

[6] *The Statesman* (California State College, Bakersfield), October 1972, p. 5.

are irrelevant. What matters is the fact that people—of all sorts—found something different in his many styles that they could enjoy and respect, not just musically but professionally as well. Dylan is considered a landmark.

Now a group of four Canadians and one American— The Band—is fast earning that same reputation. It's held by only a handful today.

Oddly enough, The Band (then known as The Hawks) was once THE band behind Dylan. It wasn't until after they parted in 1968, however, that they came into their own. Their first album (recorded while The Band was still with Dylan) received uncharacteristic praise by members of the industry. Their second album became a gold record.

At a time when most people were grooving to the static of Steppenwolf and The Vanilla Fudge, The Band began converting others to the idea of music as something other than a catalyst for dancing or a mind blower. Writing songs that seemed to identify with the Southern Reconstruction period, The Band introduced instrumental arrangements and stylistic harmonies which, when combined with the earthiest lyrics, made weary-eared listeners sit up and take notice.

"The Weight" and "The Night They Drove Old Dixie Down," both written by Jamie Robertson, are the only songs by The Band which have been made hits by other artists so far. Too few from an industry that knows them well.

At any rate, they are just getting warmed up. After four albums in as many years, The Band is breaking into new territories.

Last year's album *Cahoots* (SMAS-651) found them experimenting with intricate instrumental harmonies and entirely different lyrical themes. At a time when other composition-oriented groups seem to be dying on the vine, The Band is still developing. They can pour a unique energy into the most potentially dominating instruments and still create almost perfect blends every time. Not surprising, really, when you consider that they have all been serious musicians since they were in their early teens.

Their newest release, *Rock of Ages,* is a culmination of those four super-creative years. Recorded live at The Academy of Music in New York last New Year's Eve, this double album presents The Band and friends—with a cameo by Dylan—celebrating the end of a successful past.
In doing so, they celebrate the anticipation of an exciting future. So do we.

Rock of Ages, by means of Allen Toussaint's dynamic horn arrangements, presents the gems of the previous albums with even greater brilliance.

The final set, a tight rendition of the late Chuck Willis' "I Don't Wanna Hang Up My Rock and Roll Shoes," clearly indicates that The Band intends to keep right on moving.
A few new songs in the program confirm it.

Dylan is eternal. He has withstood every musical "movement."

The Band should too, if the past is any indication.
It's just a matter of time before this group's strength is recognized. When it is, you'll know The Band has written, and will continue to write, the rock of ages. Listen with faith—and be converted.

This writer clearly identifies his critical standards. His first two paragraphs describe Bob Dylan as a landmark, establishing him as a standard for judging other musicians. Dylan's strength is the stylistic variety of his repertoire—a characteristic shared by The Band. The repeated comparisons of Dylan and the rock group help to unify the essay. The review is more than an extended comparison, however. Several artistic qualities of the rock group are noted. The writer praises The Band's unique energy, intricate harmonies, and distinctive lyrical themes. All these aesthetic judgments are discussed in a historical context. The critic identifies some of the sources of the music (Southern Reconstruction) and the characteristics of the group's earlier albums. He also distinguishes The Band's talents and techniques from those of other contemporary rock groups.

In the next paper, a student critically analyzes a short poem by Donald Justice. Her discussion is much more detailed and somewhat more formal in tone than the previous reviews.

POEM TO BE READ AT 3 A.M. [7]

Excepting the diner
On the outskirts
The town of Ladora
At 3 A.M.
Was dark but
For my headlights
And up in
One second-story room
A single light
Where someone
Was sick or
Perhaps reading
As I drove past
At seventy
Not thinking
This poem
Is for whoever
Had the light on

AN INTERPRETATION OF
"POEM TO BE READ AT 3 A.M."

The knowledge explosion of the twentieth century has
resulted in a proliferation of startling facts concerning the
scope of the universe, and even the nature of the very protein
substances of which life is made. Science has explored new
realms of consciousness and intellect in an effort to learn
more about the human mind. Despite these vital advances
in knowledge, contemporary society has produced several
generations of compulsive souls who live out their dim,
myopic lives in loneliness. It is important then, for someone
to explore "naked life" at its most intense moments, and
to give us the feel of it, since so many people are incapable
of grasping it themselves. This task is accomplished by

[7] Donald Justice, *Night Light* (Middletown, Conn.: Wesleyan University Press, 1967). Copyright © 1967 by Donald Justice. Reprinted by permission of Wesleyan University Press.

the poets—who demonstrate the momentousness of life's most commonplace happenings. If it is only through religion that we may be *convinced* of the ultimate significance of the human scene, poetry and the other arts can at least give us a *sense* of its significance, its momentousness.

A brief poem of just eighteen lines entitled "Poem to Be Read at 3 A.M." by Donald Justice recalls an experience, and yet is an experience in itself, ready to be vicariously lived by any sensitive person who is receptive to its power of suggestion.

A most outstanding feature of the poem is the manner in which a nocturnal car trip through a remote country region is reinforced by rapid meter and careful word selection. The poet recalls his feeling of isolation as he speeds past a tiny town in which just two lights are burning. The poem is appropriately constructed in free verse with no particular rhythmic pattern present. Rhyme is chiefly used to link lines together into larger masses of continuous rhythm and meaning which the meters of individual lines help to create. "Poem to Be Read at 3 A.M.," however, contains no large portions of meaning that require a specific rhyme scheme. The lines slip easily by with no line containing more than three or four words. The steady motion of the car trip is further facilitated by the absence of those annoying stop signs otherwise collectively known as punctuation!

In keeping with the theme of swift travel through a village, it is interesting to note that the movement of verb tenses progresses from the past to the present. The poet-narrator begins the description of his mental event (traveling), and in so doing leads the reader from the past to the last three lines, in which we arrive in the present much as a car arrives at its final destination:

> This poem
> Is for whoever
> Had the light on

Thus we experience the poet's feeling of conclusion, as we reach his dedication to the unknown someone whose light he saw as he sped by on the road.

The logic of particular words within "Poem to Be Read at 3 A.M." is significant to the meaning of the poem in its entirety. The town of Ladora, through which the narrator leads us, is a small town in Iowa, with a population of 307! It is approximately twenty-five miles from Des Moines; close enough to afford its inhabitants some semblance of convenience, yet far enough removed to be among a cluster of little townships connected to one another by a network of winding country roads. The poem is intended to be read at 3 A.M. and also refers to a car trip through Ladora at 3 A.M. The hour of 3 A.M. is neatly sandwiched between 2 A.M., which calls to mind evening activities that may still be concluding, and 4 A.M., which suggests the coming of dawn. 3 A.M. is a perfectly isolated, hollow hour of the night, when darkness seems to be the deepest. The "second-story room" in which a single light burns increases the loneliness of the evening, for it is more remote and inaccessible than a first floor window would be. Inside the room someone is "sick or / Perhaps reading." Both of these events are necessarily removed from companionship. When one is sick, he is alone in his body with his sickness. Reading is likewise a solitary experience, which requires concentration in order to reap the benefits of the printed pages. Thus, it would not do to ponder on someone visiting with another in the lighted room. The driver speeds through Ladora at "seventy" miles an hour, a rather accelerated rate if one hopes to see anything but a fleeting glimpse of the scenery.

There are three images of light within "Poem to Be Read at 3 A.M." The "diner / On the outskirts" is a deserted all-night restaurant that reinforces the fact that nearly everyone is home, asleep at 3 A.M. The headlights of the car illuminate the country road as the narrator pushes on through the night. The "single light" in the second-story room is particularly lonesome. One lamp or one light bulb can do little to illuminate a dwelling full of darkness, much less the consuming darkness of the outside environs. Together or individually, these three small images of light can do little to comfort the poet, who feels alone in a world of black

night. The poet reaches out to the stranger in the room, in
the brief moment before he leaves Ladora behind. The
stranger will never know he has been beckoned, but the
reader senses the message, as the theme of loneliness
reveals itself through the growing pattern of selected words.
  "Poem to Be Read at 3 A.M." and countless other
poems of artists everywhere are unique verbal designs. They
leave us with a special sense of knowing the imperceptible
levels of emotion that unite us in our humanity, despite
the immense distances of space and time that technology
has revealed to us.

This paper is written from both an aesthetic and social perspective.
The writer gives careful attention to an analysis of the rhyme
scheme, meter, punctuation, language, and setting of the poem,
but she also interprets the work in the context of twentieth-century
technology. In her first and last paragraphs she describes the
social perspective from which she views the poem. The introductory paragraph may be a bit overwhelming for so short a paper.
But the writer's fluent style sets a brisk pace for the analysis and
her engaging personal voice sustains our interest in the paper. She
is not flip, but she is not deadly serious either.
    Professional critics often adopt a humorous or satiric tone.
In the next selection, which was published in *Newsweek,* the
writer's tone is sharp and witty.

KUNG FOOLISHNESS[8]

You have been preoccupied, of course, with the TV specials:
memorial services for two ex-Presidents, the inauguration
of a live one, the transcendence of Lance Loud, Henry
Kissinger's incredible stand-up performance as the leading
actor in a continuing dramatic series, George Foreman versus
Howard Cosell—what novelist Julio Cortazar calls "the
ordinary routine of buses and history"—and so you have
probably missed the first several episodes of "Kung Fu."

[8] Cyclops, *Newsweek,* 12 February 1973, p. 51. Copyright Newsweek, Inc.
1973, reprinted by permission.

"Kung Fu" is ABC's Thursday-night alternative to "Iron-side," at least until reruns begin next month. (Yes, reruns begin in March; a TV season is roughly the length of a football season.) "Kung Fu" features David Carradine as an Oriental monk who, for no discernible reason, wanders around the nineteenth-century American West delivering babies and being insulted—an ambulatory amalgam, I suppose, of night-school notions about Buddha, Confucius, and Lao-tse.

He is afflicted with flashbacks to when he was a hairless little tyke in the cave of his Masters, getting wise. His conversation is 120-proof Old Guru, platitudes that are the Eastern equivalent of "A rolling stone gathers no moss." His temperament, naturally, is pacifistic, although, just as naturally, he is capable of upholstering a mean karate chop whenever a baddie tries to lean on him. And whatever he does is recorded by the artiest camera work on television today: every scene seems to have been shot from the least likely angle—between the legs of a horse, from a blimp, through a mulberry bush, lush and painterly.

Paladin, Meet Ghandi

There is no excuse for any of this. It is as though the producers had been caught, naked, in a retirement home for old clichés when the fire alarm went off, and as they ran toward the exit, they grabbed whatever came to hand whether it fit or not: nonviolence, Eastern wisdom, Old West, Charlie-Chan-meet-Jimmy-Stewart-meet-Paladin-meet-Ghandi. What will it be next season—a black homosexual dwarf ex-cop, adept in voo-doo, with a liberated female mongoose as his side-kick?

Perfectly respectable actors and a lot of money have been wasted on "Kung Fu," and I am saddened the way I was saddened to learn that the giant panda isn't a bear, but a raccoon; or to learn that the nipples in the photographs in the slick girlie magazines are made erect by applying ice to the breasts of the bunnies. I am saddened that a fine actor like William Conrad is trapped, on "Cannon," in plots dreamed up by empty Coke bottles; that a fine actress like Nita Talbot is held hostage in a foofaraw of piffle like "Here We Go Again."

It just isn't that hard to make a good action-adventure series. Given the number of respectable, unemployed actors around, all that's required is a band of decent writers and an appreciation for the curiosity of the TV-watching audience. Look at any given episode of the best action series playing right now, "Hawaii Five-O." Look at last week's episode, for example. Jack Lord is never going to be Paul Newman or Robert Redford; James MacArthur is never even going to be Mickey Rooney. But their plots are as intricate as expensive watches. You learn something. Last week you learned exactly why certain stolen stocks and bonds are "negotiable" and untraceable. You learned how the market operates in a place as far away from the Big Board as Honolulu. And you saw the mastermind undone by a surprising yet completely plausible detail that he had neglected, a detail that became significant because of what you had lately learned about stocks and bonds.

So That's How It's Done

This sort of story appeals to us in the same way as Ross MacDonald's writing about "black money" or Emma Lathen's writing about fried-chicken franchises, with a little murder thrown in. We like inside information, cram courses in other people's social reality, institutional lowdown, the mechanics of a situation. ("So *that's* how it's done.") It is the basic appeal of the few flourishing popular fiction forms today: detective novels, science-fiction novels, pornography and Arthur Hailey. As our "serious" novelists came down with a terminal case of solipsism, our appetite for facts had to look elsewhere at mealtime. It looks particularly to television.

"Star Trek" knew this in its early years. We wanted an idea of what alien life and culture might be like. When "Star Trek" started to coast on the personalities of the shipmates, it died in Mr. Nielsen's arms. Character is not enough, as Peter Falk will soon find out. Faced with the same

old shuffle and twinge, week after week, the mind begins
to wander, to meditate on such irrelevancies as who better
exemplifies the spirit of twerpiness loose in the land—
Dean Martin or Mark Spitz—and the feet begin to snore.

You may feel that the commentary on "Kung Fu" is unnecessarily harsh. Yet the writer's ridicule is not random or unsupported. He attacks specific aspects of the program—the unrealistic premise, the trite dialogue, the inconsistent characterization, and the poor camera work. As a contrast he also points out qualities of a good television adventure program. His critical standards are clearly evident in his discussion of "Hawaii Five-O" and in his concluding paragraphs. The essay is written in a brisk colloquial style that easily holds our interest.

We said earlier that you can write criticism in a wide variety of styles. The next paper is a serious, analytical discussion of a short story. The student writer supports her critical views by referring regularly to specific events and descriptive details in the story. Notice too that her critical perspective is clearly expressed in the opening paragraph.

THE OTHER SIDE OF THE HEDGE

E. M. Forster's "The Other Side of the Hedge" *symbolically* emphasized the undesirable (in Mr. Forster's opinion), fast-paced competition of today's world. He describes his highway of life as an oppressive road with "dust under foot and brown crackling hedges on either side." The other side of the hedge "was green . . .—its roots showed through the clear water, and fish swam about in them—and it was wreathed over with dog-roses and Traveller's Joy." It's decidedly a much more appealing and aesthetic sight than the dusty, gravelly road. The "Traveller's Joy" also suggests that the followers of the road have been destined to arrive at this oasis. By depicting the world of progress, specialization, and competition as a dry, exhausting, monotonous road, Forster underscores the fruitlessness of such a life. His analogy of a calm, easy-paced, nontechnological world as a green, fertile, pleasant valley stresses his approval of such an existence.

Measurement is made of distances in years rather than miles as time is of prime importance in this story. The runner gauges his success in terms of years rather than miles covered, while time on the other side of the hedge is emphasized if only for the lack of it. The road itself is such a maze of windings and curves, that measurement of miles would serve no useful purpose. The milestone is not used as a device to mark miles as such, but to plot man's progress, and, as employed by the main character, to provide a resting place for those who have tired of continually plodding forward. Ironically, in the context of this story, this milestone also relies on its other meaning, that of a "significant event," as the traveller's life certainly is drastically altered by his decision to stop and rest his weary body upon this rock.

The deep pool lying on the other side of the hedge symbolizes rebirth and refreshment, as unsuspecting persons are revived and invigorated after their brisk dunking. Significantly, this purging precedes confrontation with the new life of simplicity and fraternity, just as ritualistic baptism foregoes acceptance into a religious congregation.

The scythe and the rudimentary industries of the people on the other side of the hedge testify to the pristine beauty and happiness not destroyed by technology. Their instruments and occupations were considered primitive by the people of the road, whose creed is "Every achievement is worthless unless it is a link in the chain of development." These two views seem irreconcilable, necessitating the scraping off of all the things carried by the people pushing through the hedge. The tearing of their clothes signifies the shedding of their preconceived ideas of happiness and their goal in life. The dip into the pool further accomplishes this need of starting fresh.

The "man of fifty or sixty—just the kind of age we mistrust on the road" symbolizes knowledge attained through experience. Ironically, he would receive that same distrusting reaction from many of our contemporaries, as we today glance warily at "anyone over 29." Forster has effectively captured this seemingly universal suspicion of youth for its elders through the use of this older man as a "porter" or "St. Peter" figure of the other side of the hedge.

The gates of ivory and of horn draw upon *The Odyssey* for their origin. In this classic, Penelope dreams of a gate of ivory which admits only false dreams. In contrast, she envisions a gate of horn which admits only dreams of truth. It is through the gate of ivory "that humanity went out countless ages ago, when it was first seized with the desire to walk." Thus, man was pursuing false dreams when he left his peaceful valley behind him and ventured out into the road at such an early age. He wasn't conscious of the falseness of his dreams, however. From elementary school through graduate studies, the educational system impressed upon him the value of competition and specialization. Miss Eliza Dimbleby serves as a satiric example of an expounder of this school of thought. Ironically, and perhaps comfortingly, she appears on the other side of the hedge. Forster apparently sees a ray of hope yet for our school system today. The gate of horn, the gate of true dreams, lies at the end of the road. Those who pass through will realize their total happiness can only be found beyond its entrance.

The wrenching of the can of beer-like liquid out of the man's hand at the close of the story not only signifies physical nourishment for the traveller, but also a satisfying of his appetite for meaning in his life. After refusing to accept the people's gifts of food and flowers, he catches sight of his dusty, monotonous road through the gate, and only then does he lose his self-control. He realizes the emptiness of his former life and wants to be part of this new existence. He thus lunges after the man and drinks not only from his can, but from his philosophy and life as well. This can also have a religious connotation, with the man with the scythe and beer seen as a Christ-figure. He, too, gives nourishment to his brother—nourishment of body and soul.

The organization of this paper is logical and easy to follow. The writer begins by expressing her general interpretation of the meaning of the story. The rest of the paper is devoted to a detailed analysis of the various symbolic elements that support her conclusions. She discusses the symbolic significance of measurement, the pool, the scythe, the man of fifty, the gates of ivory and horn, and the can of beer-like liquid. She offers a clearly supported explanation for each of these, and she relates them to her interpretation of the story. Keep in mind, however, that the paper's organization does not necessarily reflect the process by which the writer formed her critical opinion. She may have begun by musing over one or two aspects of the story. Perhaps she began by considering the significance of the hedge, or the road, or the two gates. Then she may have considered whether these elements could be viewed from any consistent or unified perspective. By the time she composed the first paragraph of her final draft, she was prepared to express her considered view of the entire story.

The selections discussed in this chapter illustrate only a few styles of critical writing. You can easily find examples of criticism on a wide variety of subjects. Most weekly news magazines employ film, book, television, and music critics who write regular reviews. Magazines dealing with sports, politics, food, hobbies, gardening, or fashion also publish critical essays. You might want to look at some professional journals or books to find critical articles on specialized topics.

You will probably discover, if you read one critic's reviews regularly, that even professional critics are biased in their judgment. One theater critic may consistently favor avant-garde productions while disparaging musical comedies. Another may consistently berate television dramas. Most critics, however, attempt to justify their taste by supporting their views and communicating their opinions clearly. You might find it interesting to look for two conflicting critical reviews of a book or film and consider the different critical standards and approaches that are either implicit or explicit in each essay.

I have been saying in this chapter that criticism is never wholly objective. Critical views of the same subject will differ because the critics themselves differ. Each brings his or her own individual experience, taste, and standards to the subject. As you write your own critical papers, you will want to consider carefully the criteria that guide your views. You need not agree with other critics; you may develop and express your own opinions. But you also have a critical commitment to view your topic as fully and as accurately as possible.

SPECIFIC WRITING POSSIBILITIES

Write a critical evaluation of one or more of your own papers.

Write a critical evaluation of this book.

After attending a campus event, interview others who attended and write a critical review.

Evaluate a work or phenomenon from two different critical perspectives.

Write a review of the television program you most like or least like.

Critically evaluate a film, literary work, painting, or other work of art.

Write a critical paper that discusses the social or psychological relevance of a cartoon or comic strip.

Write a critical paper about television, newspaper, or magazine advertisements.

Write a paper that expresses your aesthetic response to a building, a style of furniture, a current clothes fashion, an automobile design, or some other phenomenon.

Write a humorous criticism of social customs on your campus or in your hometown.

toward fiction

I do not intend in this chapter to offer a miniature course in fiction writing, but rather, as the title suggests, I hope to point the way from autobiography toward fiction. As I suggested earlier, various forms of writing (characterization, autobiography, fiction, and so on) often overlap—one merging into the other—so that it is not always easy to clearly distinguish one from the other. It is possible, however, to indicate a progression between these forms and to suggest some of the more significant differences between autobiographical writing and fiction.

One of the most fundamental differences is that autobiography is true and fiction is untrue. The distinction may be a misleading oversimplification, however, for fiction has its roots in the actual world, even though it may not accurately depict actual characters, events, or places. A writer's personal experience is a rich source for fiction. Your earlier writings may provide you with ideas for several stories. Beginning writers, especially, profit by drawing directly on their personal experience—the material they know best. Sometimes novice fiction writers, reluctant to reveal their own lives, try to invent a story having no relationship to their own experience. This often results in a mechanical or conventional story that has little depth or significance. Your earlier writing experiences in this course have hopefully made you sufficiently comfortable so that you can draw on your own experience with relative ease.

Although the material you use should be in some way familiar, you will also want to remember that directly communicating your specific experience is not the ultimate end in fiction. Fiction is untrue in the sense that its primary purpose is not the communication of literally true facts or events. Fiction writing requires you to transform your experience—to reshape it into a literary work. In earlier chapters you have had opportunities to include a variety of writing techniques in your papers. We have discussed interior monologue, dialogue, direct and indirect characterization, dramatization, use of setting, various organizations, and the need for a central focus in your papers. All these techniques or elements are also important in fiction writing. In fact, the writer's control and integration of these elements is perhaps more important in fiction. This may be one of the crucial distinctions between autobiographical writing and fiction. When the shaping and integration of various writing elements into a well-formed work take precedence over the factual content of the paper, you are crossing over from autobiography to fiction. In fiction the art of the story is more important than fact. You might defend an autobiographical paper by saying "That's the way it really happened," but such a defense is not valid for a fiction story. In fiction actual facts are routinely sacrificed for the form of the story as a whole. The characters, setting, action, tone, and point of view must fit together to form a unified literary work.

Perhaps the first step in reshaping an autobiographical paper into fiction is a psychological one. I encouraged you earlier to detach yourself at least partially from the experiences you wrote about. I emphasized the importance of being both "in" and "out" of an experience at the same time. When you write fiction, you will want to detach yourself even further from your own experience. You will need to stop regarding the experience as a true incident or actual relationship that must be accurately preserved. In order to transform or metamorphize your actual experience, you will have to stop thinking of the experience as an inviolate part of your past and begin to regard it as raw material that will be cut up, partially discarded, and pasted together with new material to form a literary work that may have only a slight resemblance to your life.

Once you have sufficiently detached yourself from the experience, you will want to consider the central focus and the point of view (or means of perception) and the organization of the story. As a personal essay your paper may have focused on your relationship with your mother and father, but as a fiction story you may want to focus primarily on the child, on the mother, or on the father. When you consider this matter, you will also want to consider whose story it will be. Who is the central character? Is it the father's story? The mother's? Because of its limitations in length a short story usually focuses on only one character. Novels, of course, can deal in more depth with several characters.

Some sample student papers will aid our discussion of focus, organization, and point of view in fiction. The following paper was written as an autobiographical essay. This selection is particularly suitable for our purposes because the author later rewrote it as fiction.

A PERSONAL ESSAY

A half hour had now passed since I had the kids dressed and ready. They waited impatiently and began to get on each other's nerves. Alex screamed no at Holly about every ten seconds, it seemed, and I tried to remind myself that the "terrible twos" would pass inevitably. Holly struggled against his noise while cutting out paper dolls on the uneven surface of the nubby carpet. My fingers leafed through last week's *TV Guide* while I pondered whether to toss Alex in bed for a while. Finally, I lost interest and looked down on Sunday's listings to see what I had missed on Glen Campbell. The house had not cooled down from earlier and sweat oozed down my forehead, through my eyebrows, and onto the top of my eyelids. I had spent a lot of time trying to get the eyeliner on even and the shadow subtly hued. What a waste! We had expected him over a half hour ago. Why does he always pull this?

The house was spotless and neatly settled, rather unlike how it used to be when he lived with us. The dishes were even put away. I'm not sure why it had to be just so, but that's the way I wanted it. The living room furniture was changed, and I knew he would feel estranged not only from us after all this time, but from the whole environment. He had never seen us in this house. I wondered if he would feel at all a part of us here. My parents had helped out by giving me some of my grandmother's furniture—a chair,

lamp, drum table—as well as about $1,000 of their own
to replace what we had lost.

Now another twenty minutes was gone. Good grief. I got
up to get a cigarette and my nail file. The kids continued
to hassle. Pretty soon it would be their bedtime. Back on
the couch, I tried to shape my nails. God. They're so ugly.
And hangnails that won't quit. I never see other women with
such bad looking cuticles. They look as though I ran my
fingers through a food grater. God, where is he? The same
old pattern seemed to emerge again. His actions and stories
I think are permanently delineated on my mind. My thoughts
always the same: "Where in the hell is he this time?"
"John, are you coming home tonight?" "I'm so tired of this,
so tired." Then he'd come home finally. "Sorry I'm late, baby.
We got to bullshitting over at Carl's, and I forgot." Sometimes he brought sweet rolls with him if it were in the
morning. I'd forget for a while. We were priest and supplicant
repeating liturgy at each other every day for five and one half
years until finally, the benediction. Why does he have to
come? It's such a farce.

I stopped filing my nails and began to daydream. There
I was, sitting in his old vinyl black recliner that lived with
us once in married housing. Last year; last June even.
Sitting in that chair, rocking; then shifting gears and reclining
all the way back. I stared through the window into the
languorous twilight of early summer. The quiet, nostalgic
sounds of neighbors chatting outside before armies of
mosquitos drove them in. The thunderous bong of each
stair, like an untuned xylophone, when someone ran down
the iron stairwell outside from the balcony. The occasional
screech of a child as he leaped into the bathtub to bubble
away the day's accumulated filth. And I waited. The outside
noises now dissipated with the day. A breeze came up.
Suddenly I saw palms in the front yard where those ugly
black locusts had been. The surrounding buildings became
a sprawling lakeside motel. The air was full with the cool,
fresh smell of a nearby lake. I remember this image appeared
to me every night in the summer. Then it would pass.
I continued to wait.

187

Now I interrupted my daydream to look down at my thumbnail. I deliberated. Unless it's ragged or torn, I avoid working on that nail because it always seems thicker to me. It requires more time. Then, finally, John knocked at the door. I knew it was him; I guess I knew it instinctively. Holly ran to the door yelling, "Daddy, Daddy," and after she opened it, jumped at him and hugged his thighs unrelentingly. Alex ran to the door, too, but quickly withdrew and held his gaze on the floor.

John glowed at Holly's reception. Patting away her head, he approached Alex cautiously. "Hiya, Tiger. Man, has he grown." A smile flashed on his face as he saw me beyond. "Hey, Baby, you're looking fine these days." Then he surveyed the room lightly. "You seem to be doing all right for yourself. I knew your old man would come through."

He sat down in my grandmother's chair and crossed his legs. "It's nice. I don't see any of the old stuff. Say, what do you have to pay here a month?" Then he forgot the question. "Hey, Baby, sorry I'm late, but you know. Things came up. No matter how hard I try. Couldn't get Teddy to drive me over to East Lansing 'cause he was supposed to go to work at five, so I waited on Wesley for a ride. He was at Teddy's. But that mother wanted to stop in at Grandmother's to see Herm. He's in town this weekend, too. Anyways, while we were in there, I saw this guy I met at Sweet's place one day, and borrowed his car. In fact, I gotta pick him up at his girl's house in about an hour. Which reminds me, while I think of it, I want to use your phone. I'm going to Detroit tomorrow morning and I gotta call Jesse. I'm gonnna borrow his car if his old lady isn't gonna use it."

He pulled his little book out of his back pocket as he walked into the kitchen. Holly picked up her scissors again and started cutting out dolls. Alex grabbed the nail file out of my lap and tried to file his toenails. And I got up to make a cup of coffee out of the tap and returned to my *TV Guide*.

The writer here is depicting a marital relationship at a moment of intensity that clarifies her perception of the marriage. We learn about the narrator, her husband, their children, and about their mutual relationship as a family. The central focus is on the writer. Most of all it is her story, and of course it is filled with her perspectives and biases. At times, in fact, her bias may be too obvious. John's behavior, for example, seems to justify the writer's earlier responses to him—perhaps, in fact, he behaves so predictably as to arouse our suspicion. Not all her comments are so obvious, however. The narrator's final statement subtly and efficiently communicates her ultimate rejection of the relationship and the marriage. She would rather drink coffee made from tap water and read the *TV Guide* than continue the meaningless encounter with her husband.

In order to transform this experience into fiction, the writer had to detach herself from the encounter and consider what alterations in focus, point of view, and structure were needed to shape a story. First of all, she had to decide whose story it would be. It could remain the wife's story, or it could become the husband's or even the children's story.

Another matter the writer had to consider was the point of view, or means of perception, of the story. Through whose eyes should the story be told? A story can be told in the first person by either the central character or a minor character. As a personal experience this paper focuses on the wife and is related by her. If the writer chooses to keep this point of view when she writes the experience as a fiction story, she has to keep in mind that the first-person voice in fiction differs from the first-person voice in autobiography. The narrator in autobiography is actually the writer. In fiction, however, the first-person narrator is not the writer, but a persona—a fictional person created by the writer. By creating a persona the writer of fiction is able to become removed from the experience being related. Of course, the story could be told in the first person by the husband, or it could focus on the children and be told by one of them. It could also focus on the wife but be told by a child, by the husband, or even by a neighbor.

Another possibility would be to tell the story in the third-person point of view, which can be handled in a variety of ways. Many stories are told from a limited third-person viewpoint. This means of perception may be the easiest approach for you if you are a novice at fiction writing. A limited third-person viewpoint will enable you to distance yourself from your own experience.

The voice will remind you that the material is no longer your life but is merely the raw stuff for a story that is indeed not factual. All the student stories in this chapter use this means of perception. The writer uses the third-person voice but also reveals the thoughts and feelings of the central character; the thoughts of no other characters are revealed, however. To rewrite "A Personal Essay" in a limited third-person voice the writer could name the wife, and change *I* to *she*. Since the essay delves only into the narrator's thoughts, the writer could switch fairly easily from first person to third person. Another possibility would be to tell the story in the third person but reveal only the husband's thoughts or only a neighbor's thoughts. It is also possible to tell a story in the third person without revealing the thoughts of any character. Very few stories are told in this objective third-person voice. You may want to read Shirley Jackson's "The Lottery" and Irvin Shaw's "The Girls in Their Summer Dresses," two professional examples written from an objective point of view.

Finally, the writer of "A Personal Essay" might choose to write her story from an omniscient point of view, dipping into the thoughts of several characters. This approach is no longer used as much as it once was. One modern example of omniscient viewpoint is Ernest Hemingway's "The Short Happy Life of Francis Macomber." In this story Hemingway relates the thoughts of Macomber, his guide Wilson, and even some thoughts attributed to a lion. The possible choices in point of view are extensive. If you are not sure what viewpoint is best suited to your story, you might experiment by rewriting the story from several different viewpoints.

When the author of the earlier autobiography later rewrote the paper as a short story, she decided to keep the focus on the wife, but to narrate the story from a limited third-person point of view. The wife Anne doesn't directly tell the story, but the reader sees the experience from Anne's perspective and learns what Anne's thoughts are. The change in point of view is perhaps the most obvious alteration, but you also will notice other significant changes in this version.

THE LOVERS

A half hour had passed since Anne had the kids dressed and ready. They waited impatiently and the smaller one now

vocalized his intolerance. Timmy screamed no at Karen
every few seconds as she struggled to cut out paper flowers
on the carpet. Anne tried to remind herself that he would
be out of this stage eventually. Her fingers leafed through
last week's *TV Guide* as she pondered whether to take him
to his room and read him a story. Finally, she lost interest
in the possibility and looked down Sunday's listings to
see what she had missed on Glen Campbell. The house
had not cooled down from earlier, and sweat drained down
her forehead through the brows and onto her eyelids. She had
spent twenty minutes trying to get the eyeliner and eyebrow
pencil on evenly, and her efforts seemed wasted. He had
been expected over a half hour ago.

Anne got up from the couch, went into the bathroom,
and examined her face. The eyebrows had faded. She took
the pencil out of the medicine cabinet and stroked them
in more distinctly. There, that was better. She looked down at
the green knit dress, but it still looked fresh.

"Mommy. Timmy is taking my flowers and he's tearing
them apart."

"No." Timmy's voice echoed with defiance in hearing
his name used harshly.

"Well, Timmy, leave Karen's things alone. Go play with
your horse." Anne went into her bedroom to get the nail file
from her dresser drawer but stopped when she caught a
glimpse of herself in the mirror. Maybe a little more lipstick,
she thought. She dabbed some on her lower lip. There.
That was better. Her blue eyes gazed at the blond image in
the mirror. It looked much sleeker now, the limbs more taut
and better proportioned. She was reassured.

"Mommy." Karen called loudly now, emphasizing each
word. "Timmy's still doing it."

"For God sakes, you two. Cut it out and stop fighting.
Your father will be here soon." At least hopefully he will
be, she thought. It had occurred to her that he might not
show up at all.

Anne lay down on the bed and tried to make sense of
what was happening to her. He had sounded so urgent
on the phone as though he had to speak with her immediately.
He had stammered out the words painfully, and she had

acquiesced, sensing a familiar involvement reemerging. Yet now he was an hour overdue. Why couldn't he just once be there, and be on time, she asked herself. He had said it was very important. She curled up hugging the pillow and let her feet hang from the side of the bed, her shoes dangling. She began to recount their courtship and how they had married so fast against much parental opposition. She knew her motives were more than rebellion. There had been something very exciting and dynamic about him. She had felt that he could do anything superbly and had bragged to her friends about him. Ed had not been typical in any way, and she had been crazy about him.

A shriek interrupted her thoughts. "Now what's going on?"

Timmy ran into the bedroom and pointed to his arm. "Mommy, see?"

"What's the matter?" There was a long bloodless scratch on his arm. "Well, it'll be all better soon." She touched her lips to the arm. "Now go on and play. Karen, put those scissors away before somebody gets hurt again." Timmy ran off to the living room.

She stared at the drapes and saw they weren't closed yet. Yes, she had loved him. And she thought that he even had genuinely loved her at one time. Why else would he have gotten married, a man like that. No one had thought him the type for marriage, and she remembered how surprised his friends were when they announced it. She slid across the bed and pulled the cord, yanking the drapes together. He had even lived with several girls, so she knew he had felt differently toward her. She found it hard to understand why they had not been happy. Perhaps even now there was something left.

Then Karen stood at the door with tears in her eyes. She was holding the remnants of paper flowers. "Mommy, Timmy spoiled it. It's just ruined."

"Dammit." Anne got up and went into the living room and grabbed Timmy's shoulders, shaking him. "Why do you have to pester Karen so much? Can't you leave her alone?" Timmy sobbed fitfully and tears ran down his cheeks.

Anne became angrier. "Don't you realize what you've done?" His eyes looked up at her softly and now she realized that he was overtired. Her voice mellowed. "Go on, now, and play in your room. Play with your truck—or look at a book. Come on and get busy and stay out of here."

She bent over to help Karen pick up the rest of the torn paper. Karen sat crosslegged, her back slumped over, listlessly fingering a yellow petal. Anne touched her shoulder. "It was very beautiful. Try and make another one, honey. It might even turn out prettier than this."

"Oh, Mommy. I wanted it to be this one. It was for Daddy. I can't make another one before he comes."

Anne's voice grew heavier. "Well, there might be time. You know your father. He's already very late."

Karen left the room and brought back more colored paper. Anne sat down on the couch but then remembered the nail file was still in her drawer. She walked down the hall to her room, passing the children's room as she did. She saw Timmy was playing with the buggy. After getting the file, she returned to the couch and began to shape her nails. Her face grimaced as she saw how ragged her cuticles looked. It seemed to her that somehow she must have caught her hands in a food grater, because there were so many hangnails. Her thoughts drifted. Everything tonight seemed so familiar, a pattern so sharply cut that it was etched permanently in her mind. All her thoughts had been the same. She knew that when he came his words would be predictable: "Sorry I'm late, Baby. We got to bullshitting and I forgot." Or, "I ran out of gas and couldn't find a station open." Yet sometimes his stories were so strange or complicated she found it hard not to believe him. When he came in after the stores opened in the morning, he would bring sweet rolls. Once in a while, he'd take her out for dinner or to a show if she could find a babysitter. He wanted to help her forget. He had said he could understand how she felt, but he couldn't change things until they were ready to leave married housing. Then he planned to take them out West, find a job, and buy a house. He had too many friends here and it would be impossible before then.

If he's coming here to tell me that he wants us now
and that we don't have to wait any more, I don't want to hear
it, she thought. She clenched her fists and tightened her
arms. Then she looked down at her nails. They were finished
except for the one long thumbnail. Thumbnails she felt
were harder to manage because they were thicker and
required more time. Her hands began to perspire, and the
task now seemed too tedious. Did he intend to suggest that?
She realized he had already closed the door tonight without
even being aware.

The clock on the bookcase showed ten. Anne looked
over at Karen. The new bouquet was nearly complete. Timmy
was quiet. Anne decided to see if he was still playing. As she
entered the room, she saw him sprawled out in a little bed
he had made for himself on the floor with Karen's blanket
and pillow. He slept clutching a Dr. Suess book. She turned
and left, leaving the light on. The memories closed in now
more tightly. This is how it had always been. The old black
chair of his appeared now, and she grew bitter. She
remembered sitting in it quietly rocking, then later shifting
gears and reclining all the way back. She had stared through
the front windows, but the focus was too narrow. The
languorous twilight of early summer; the quiet, nostalgic
sounds of neighbors chatting before armies of mosquitos
drove them in; the thunderous bong of each stair like an
untuned xylophone when someone ran down the iron stairwell
outside from the balcony; the occasional screech of a child
as he leaped into the bathtub to bubble away the day's
accumulated filth. Then the outside noises would dissipate
with the endless day. Suddenly she saw palms in the front
yard where the locusts had been. The surrounding buildings
would metamorphize into a sprawling lakeside motel. The air
would be full with the cool, fresh smell of a nearby lake.
The image became her hope, the focal point of her dreams.
Now she hated that chair. She would not think of it again.

Anne put out her cigarette and as she looked up, Karen
stood in front dangling her new bouquet. She wore a coy
smile. "Do you think this one will be ok?"

"It's lovely, Karen. You've done a very good job with

this one." There was a knock at the door as she finished speaking. Anne tightened. Karen ran for the door yelling, "Daddy, Daddy," and after she opened it, jumped at him and hugged his thighs unrelentingly. Timmy heard the commotion and came running out of his room toward the front door. When he saw Ed towering above him, he withdrew shyly and gazed at the floor.

Ed glowed at Karen's reception. Patting away her head, he approached Timmy cautiously. "Hiya, Tiger. How ya doing?" A smile flashed across his deeply tanned small face as he saw Anne beyond. "Hey, Baby, you're looking fine these days." His voice was easy, almost flippant.

He surveyed the room lightly and then sat down in the old brocade chair and crossed his legs. He wore red corduroy pants and a long, black Edwardian jacket. She thought he seemed thinner. His hair was long on top, combed back to cover its sparseness, and he had grown sideburns, trimmed below his ears. The brown eyes sparkled through fluttering eyelids. "You seem to be doing all right for yourself these days. I knew your old man would come through."

"Yes. He always does." The sharpness of her voice echoed in her ears. Her eyes shifted quickly away. It had to be done.

"It's nice here. What do you have to pay a month?"

It would be difficult. She looked back at him evenly. "Too much. I can't afford it, but I won't live in a slum either. It's $160 and I had to pay a $200 damage deposit. We probably won't even get half of that back if we ever move."

"Daddy." It was Karen. She held the flowers toward him. "Here is a present for you. It's the second one I made 'cause Timmy ripped up the other one." She looked over at Timmy triumphantly.

"Well, how nice. Thanks, honey." He put it along the side of the chair and looked back at Anne. "Have you been getting along all right? I mean, do you like your job?"

"It's a job. Very monotonous. And I can barely support us on what it pays. I don't know how the kids and I'll get by. I can never get myself to the dentist or buy new shoes or anything. You just don't know how hard it is for a woman to support herself on what people want to pay." She leaned all the way back in the couch and uncrossed her legs.

Timmy finally came close to the chair. Ed picked him up and absently placed him on his knee, bouncing him slowly. "How's Karen doing in school?"

"Well, not too good. Her teacher said she daydreams too much. I was very upset about that because Karen is so intelligent and she's already wasting it. I think she's going to turn out just like you." Anne lit a cigarette and continued. "You're awfully curious about us. Have you finally got yourself a decent, steady job?"

"I've been lining things up and talking with a few people." He took Timmy's arms and tried to get him to box. "I don't want to commit myself yet. I want them to come to me."

It was as she realized it had to be. He was too old now. "Christ, you've had a whole year out there. Can't you ever get anything done?"

"Yeah, I get things done. Not everything can be done 1-2-3. It takes time. I'm not gonna get myself stuck with some shitty job that's goin' nowhere. And don't expect me to sit at some small desk for the next forty years typing memos or time sheets. Shit." He looked down at Timmy, his face set.

"Who's asking you to do all that?"

He sat erect and glared at her. "Christ. Who the hell you think is asking? Why do you have to get on my ass?" His bullish features contorted into a sneer. "A job, a schedule, a paycheck, sitting around watching TV on Saturday nights. Go get yourself a computer, Baby. That's just what you need. I'm a man—and don't you ever forget it."

Her voice was bland. "Uh huh." Then, controlling the corners of her mouth, she looked over at Timmy. "Do you think Timmy has grown much? I can't really tell."

Ed looked at the child. "He's huge. Timmy, does your mama feed you all day long?"

"No." Timmy's eyes sparkled at him uncomprehendingly.

"He's definitely going to play football. I can see that already." Ed looked back at Anne and spoke more easily. "By the way, sorry I'm late, but you know. Things came up.

No matter how hard I try. Couldn't get Teddy to drive me
over here 'cause he was supposed to go to work at five.
So I waited on Wesley for a ride. He was at Teddy's. But
that mother wanted to stop in at Tom's Bar to see Herm.
He's in town this weekend too. Anyways, while we were in
there, I saw this guy I met at Sweet's place one day and
borrowed his car. In fact, I gotta pick him up at his girl's
house in an hour."

"Oh, you can't stay." Anne measured her words
carefully. "I thought you had something important to discuss
with me. You said, or it seemed like you said, it was urgent."
She folded her hands tightly.

"Well, it was no big thing." He spoke almost too casually.
He hesitated momentarily and then continued more smoothly.
"I wanted to find out about something but Sweet probably
can do it for me, or maybe Jesse." He looked around the
living room and then into the kitchen. "Say, can I use your
phone a minute? I want to call Jesse and see if I can use his
car tomorrow if his old lady isn't gonna take it. I'm going
to Detroit." He pulled a little red book out of his back pocket
as he walked into the kitchen to use the phone.

Karen sat on the floor fingering the bouquet of flowers
left on the seat, and Timmy grabbed the nail file off the table
and tried to file his toenails. Anne watched him quietly
as he opened the book to find the number and then pressed
the buttons to complete the call. She got up then to make
a cup of coffee out of the tap and returned to her *TV Guide.*

The intent in this version is no longer to relate a purely factual or
personal experience, but to reshape that experience so that the
fictional elements contribute to the structure and unity of the story
as a whole. More details have been included in the second draft—
details that are not accurate according to the first draft, but that
contribute depth and consistency to the characterization and the
conflict. The fiction story still focuses on the wife, but the move to
the third-person voice makes her sound less biased. You may have
noticed also that the character of Anne in the second draft differs
from the "I" in the first draft. Anne is a more rounded figure—a
character with more clarity and depth. She takes on a life of her

own. She is more in control of the situation and more perceptive about herself. Anne also admits her complicity in the unsatisfactory marriage relationship. ("She knew her motives were more than rebellion. There had been something very exciting and dynamic about him. She had felt that he could do anything superbly and had bragged to her friends about him. Ed had not been typical in any way, and she had been crazy about him.") She also demonstrates some of her own impatience with the children, rather than characterizing herself as a thoroughly dedicated parent in contrast to the father's imperceptiveness and neglect. In the second draft the characterization of the father has altered too. He is no longer simply a one-dimensional fall guy. In the first draft the narrator more or less judges the husband for us. In the second draft, however, the writer includes dialogue and other essential information that enables us as readers to draw more of our own conclusions. Notice too that the encounter between Anne and Ed is more detailed and more dynamic. The scene builds carefully to the crisis. Finally it becomes clear what the outcome both of this encounter and of the marriage will be:

"Oh, you can't stay." Anne measured her words carefully. "I thought you had something important to discuss with me. You said, or it seemed like you said, it was urgent." She folded her hands tightly.

The carefully measured words and the tightly folded hands communicate her restrained acceptance of the situation. She is in control of herself.

"The Lovers" does not significantly differ in structure from the autobiographical paper. You might want to consider ways to alter the structure of your story, however. You might organize events chronologically, use one long flashback, or use a series of flashbacks. You might even separate your story into a series of labeled parts or scenes. Short stories often focus on a specific time in the life of the central character. In each of the examples in this chapter the reader learns a great deal about the lives of the central characters, but the actual story is restricted to a few hours. Your final choice will probably be determined by which organization is best suited to the point of view, the central focus, and the characterization of your story. Often by changing one element you alter the entire story, so you may want to experiment with several possible organizations before you select one.

We mentioned earlier that a fiction writer attempts to integrate a variety of elements to produce a unified short story. The writer's choice of point of view, characterization, setting, plot, central conflict, and thematic concern are often interdependent. Each is an integral part of the story as a whole, and each is used as effectively and efficiently as possible. In "The Lovers," for example, the setting helps to reinforce the anxiety of the central character and contributes to the tension between Anne and Ed, as well as Anne's impatience with the children. The weather is hot and uncomfortable: "The house had not cooled down from earlier, and sweat drained down her forehead through the brows and onto her eyelids." The emphasis on time also helps to increase the tension of the story. The later it gets, the more irritated Anne becomes. Notice too that though the central conflict is within Anne (Does she or does she not want to live with Ed?), her tension is echoed in a series of more explicit conflicts—the children's bickering, Anne's impatience with them, her fidgeting with her nails, and finally her confrontation with Ed.

The writer of the next story also uses fictional elements efficiently. The setting, dialogue, action, and characterization all contribute to the internal conflict of the main character, Tom.

SUMMER HOLOCAUST

Gnawing the side of the yellow P A G pencil, Tom tensed up in his green chair at the kitchen table. He looked disgustedly at the ashtray full of cigarette butts and then rubbed his forehead trying to ease out his three-day-old headache. He ran his rough, hay-bitten fingers through his balding hair. The spiciness of freshly made catsup still lingered in the kitchen. "Where to from here?" he agonized.

As he rubbed his eyes the dimly lighted, cluttered kitchen faded in and out—dirty supper dishes still on the sink, the baby's toy-scattered playpen in the corner, tomato-stained towels tossed over the back of chairs, cans of bright red tomato juice and catsup lining Joanne's work table. Once in a while a Kerr lid popped as the last of them sealed. In the evening stillness, millers buzzed around the quiet light over the sink while the water faucet dripped monotonously, irritatingly. From the bedroom the baby whimpered half-heartedly as Joanne changed his diaper and sponged the day's play off his hands, face, and feet. Outside the youngsters shouted excitedly as they chased lightning bugs, trying to capture them for their quart jar prison.

In the distance, down by the pond, crickets chirped their evening lullaby while a bullfrog brazenly honked his way around the green watery edge. "Shut up," he thought futilely, "I can't stand it." He sighed unevenly, half thinking of how three days ago he had loved to listen to that familiar evening music. It punctuated the secure feeling he had, sitting inside with his feet propped up, a half-empty glass of cold beer in one hand, the *Farm Journal* in the other, relaxing one day closer to the end of the harvest season.

Angry tears began to course down Tom's rough, sunburned cheeks. His stomach muscles tightened. It felt like he'd consumed the bottom of the hard cider barrel. His teeth clenched ... "damn" ... he gripped the pencil like he would the rope of a contrary calf. He shifted in his chair, sprawling his feet in hopeless restlessness: "harvesting just about done ... only the corn to go ... best wheat crop ever ... fifty bushel to the acre ... the January price rise would have paid off the debt on the milking parlor," he mused painfully. "The straw perfectly dry—no rain to ruin it or the hay ... clever hay had touched the barn rafters," he smiled quietly, remembering how the boys had bitched when their heads banged on the rafters while they piled the bales in ... "good for 'em ... might knock some sense in 'em."

"Damn, they were right—it was piled too high. Now, nothing—start all over." In the lazy dusky atmosphere a sparrow had flown drunkenly into the lighted bulb and ignited the holocaust.

The crickets had stopped momentarily. Everything seemed tensely quiet—like the restless calmness between thunder bolts. "What could the kids be up to," he wondered. "They are too quiet."

He pricked his ears to the low whispering coming

from the front steps. He quietly slid off the chair and tiptoed to the screen door. Ten-year-old Randy, skinny, red-headed, freckled—his right-hand man this summer— folded almost in half, intent on the captured lightning bugs in the jar, sat close to nine-year-old Cindy. "Ordinarily they were as frisky as young calves first let out to pasture," Tom pondered, "but the last three days, they had tiptoed around—in their way trying to help . . . boys hate to see their dads bawl," Tom thought half in shame.

"Randy was the first one out there when the men came the next day to help clean up the rubble. He had cried desperately because his little Holstein calf—the first of his own—was in the top floor of the barn, and by the time they saw the flames shooting out the roof it was too hot and smoky to get inside," Tom remembered bitterly. "Anyway it was in behind the self-propelled combine and the new John 880 diesel tractor. The heat was so intense no one could save them. If anyone had started them up, they would have exploded. Now . . . nothing but a heap of black rubble. Damn!"

"Do you think we'll move to town, Cindy?" Randy asked, weakly shaking the lightning bug jar. "The night I stayed with Joey Thompson there wasn't nothing to do—no calves to feed . . . no ensilage to throw down . . . he can't go sparrow hunting with his BB gun . . . he can't even drive a tractor."

"Yah," muttered Cindy, intent on braiding the timothy straw she had pulled up by the steps.

"Daddy will probably give me the next new calf and I can start all over. Anyway, I'd be willin' to wait till spring, since Daddy might need to sell the bulls that come this winter to pay for the new barn," Randy continued intently. "He wouldn't sell all the cows because we don't have any place to milk them, would he?" he cried—as if Cindy were his dad.

"Randy, did you see that old mother cat today? She's just wanderin' around lost—all her kittens got burned up," Cindy complained, as if she hadn't heard Randy's last question.

"Yah, they must a been drinkin' out of the cat pan in the milkin' parlor," Randy theorized coldly.

"Gee, I was so scared—all those fire engines—men shoutin'—Mom cryin'—I didn't even think of the kittens. In Catechism, Mrs. Durbin was tellin' us what hell was like. That must be it and I'm scared," she stated determinedly.

Tom turned around and walked dumbly toward the refrigerator. The kitchen blurred again. "What a damned baby I am," he thought disgustedly. He pulled open the refrigerator door, grabbed a cold, damp can of Budweiser, angrily slammed the door shut, jarring the St. Joseph statue on the top. The can top popped with his quick, brusque pull. The beer's freshness cooled his feverish lips, throat, stomach. Less angrily he plopped himself back onto the kitchen chair, set the can down. His elbows thudded on the table top as he cupped his hands over his stubbly chin.

He stared blankly out the newly installed picture window. The savage flames seemed to shoot up from the barn roof again, as they had three nights ago when he sat down in that very place to have a late supper after helping his brother get the field chopper in shape to begin filling the silo the next day.

Tom massaged his brow. "What about Joanne? Would she really want me to sell out? If I sold all fifty Holsteins and got a decent price for the farm, I might break even," he ventured for the first time. "But, Oh, God, the house ... just remodeled ... new white siding ... a bigger kitchen ... the dishwasher she had been coaxing for ... fire insurance would help ... but who would ever finance two 300×25 silos, a milking parlor ... all my wheat, hay, straw burned to hell."

Joanne sauntered out of the bedroom—all the youngsters but Randy and Cindy in bed. Her black hair was rumpled and stringy—not the usual neat, simple just-combed look. Her faded house dress still had the tomato stains from the afternoon's work. Her usually alert, freckled face was drawn, tired from tension. Her mouth and cheeks ached from forcing a smile each time a neighbor brought food, an offer of hay, straw, or stanchions for three or four cows till things were rebuilt. In spite of herself she was moved by their thoughtfulness.

"What's the decision, Tom?" she ventured, gritting her teeth as she settled, relieved to sit down on the green and gray plastic-covered kitchen chair. Every bone in her body ached with exhaustion. Tom continued to grip the pencil—his paper had only a few meaningless numbers weakly scratched on it.

Wouldn't she ever understand? The past eleven years of bickering . . . she hated being way out in the sticks . . . cow hair made her itch . . . at first she almost vomited every time she went near the barn . . . all the vanishing cream in the world wouldn't smooth out her hands after hoeing and digging in the garden . . . she did pride herself in the one hundred quarts of frozen corn . . . now the seventy quarts of tomato juice . . . fifty pints of catsup . . . with six kids, no time for bridge . . . . "Really, Tom—you don't think you can start over now. I was almost glad to see the neighbors take the cows to board them. Why don't they just buy them?"

"Hell, Joanne, can't you ever see? Randy's been talkin' about gettin' the first calf so *he* can start over . . . ."

The afternoon flashed back through his mind—he had gone up to the roller-bearing factory because she had begged him to . . . the hot, stuffy, oily smelling assembly line . . . his head throbbed from the closeness . . . the hard, monkey-grease-smeared cement floor, the bored look on the men's gray-complexioned faces—the monotony . . . they didn't give a damn if they missed a bolt or two . . . what was it to them . . . just cogs themselves . . . never feeling the fulfillment of your own completed work . . . their lightly tanned arms flabby, bellies fat from no exercise . . . Randy would never be in shape for football . . . only the green frosted windows—an illusion of outdoor freshness. Even cow manure smelled better than the stinking heat, like burning rubber mixed with sulfur, blasting out of the roaring steel presses . . . the noise still roared in his ears . . . .

. . . but the money . . . beginning wage better than he would make for years . . . farm prices lower than ever . . . weekends to rest . . . wouldn't have to get up at 5:00 to milk . . . . "If Daddy gives me a calf I can start all over" . . .

Joanne could go to her damned bridge clubs . . . get her
hair done every week . . . .

Tom heaved a deep, exhausted sigh. He shifted in
his chair . . . his hand crept toward Joanne's stretched out
limply on the table. As he grasped her hand, Joanne felt
his agony, determination, pleading, transfer like an electrical
current. It begged strength, support. "In sickness and
health, for better or for worse, 'till death . . ."

As he looked pleadingly at her, his sunburned muscular
face taut with anguish, she reassuringly—in reflex
movement—nodded her head. A smile slowly crept across
his tense face.

He abruptly shoved back his chair, the scratching
echoing on the linoleum, startling a cricket which had
found its way inside. He reached for the phone.
5—9—9—6—8—0—4 the round dial obediently registered.

"Hello, Joe. This is Tom. I know it's after hours but
could I come over? I need your help to get a loan."

The writer accomplishes a great deal in the first paragraph of this
story. She introduces the main character and catches our interest
by only hinting at the nature of his plight. We want to know more
about Tom—why he has been smoking for three days, and why
he is so upset. The paragraph also establishes the point of view
and introduces the setting, the tone, and the story's central focus.
Tom himself poses the question, which turns out to be the central
question of the story—"Where to from here?"

Notice that the writer doesn't relate the crucial information
all at once. Instead she communicates bits and pieces as they are
needed. The first three paragraphs establish the setting and tone
and indirectly relate a great deal about Tom. He is a farmer, he is
emotionally upset, he has children, and his wife has been canning
tomatoes.

We also learn that it is an evening near the end of harvest
season, and that Tom's children are not as upset as Tom is. The
noise and clutter of the kitchen (dirty dishes, toy-scattered playpen, whimpering baby, dripping faucet) and even the night sounds
of crickets and bullfrogs all serve to intensify Tom's anxiety. Not
until the fourth and fifth paragraphs, however, do we learn the
cause of his difficulty—his barn with all the summer harvest has

burned. The conflict, however, is not simply Tom's struggle to adjust to his loss. Nor is it his indecision about whether he wants to rebuild the farm. (He is convinced he would like to try again.) The conflict, rather, as we eventually learn, is Tom's struggle to decide whether he should please himself or move to town to please his wife. In a few brief flashbacks and scattered memories we learn of Joanne's dislike of farm life and Tom's dislike of city work: "Even cow manure smelled better than the stinking heat, like burning rubber mixed with sulfur, blasting out of the roaring steel presses . . . the noise still roared in his ears. . . ."

Perhaps the weakest aspect of this story is the resolution. The details of the story have clearly informed us of Tom's emotions, distress, and desires, but we are not adequately prepared for Joanne's acquiescence. Her final agreement to stay on the farm comes a bit too quickly. Except for this weakness, the story is well-paced and effectively structured. The writer vividly describes the setting and moves smoothly from Tom's interior monologues to external dialogue. The movement from present events to memories of earlier events (the fire, the factory, Joanne's attitude) is also handled effectively.

Both of the previous stories include a variety of narrative methods—dialogue, thoughts (interior monologue), description, action, and exposition. Of the five methods, however, exposition is usually the least used in short stories. Too much exposition—direct telling of the story—can prevent the reader from becoming involved with the characters, action, and tone of the story. "Summer Holocaust," for example, could be reduced to a few sentences of exposition.

> Tom, a farmer with six children, has just lost his barn
> and summer harvest in a fire. He is discouraged but wants
> to start over. His children enjoy the farm, but his wife,
> Joanne, has not enjoyed the eleven years of farm life.
> She would like the family to move to the city. Tom has looked
> for a city job. He hates the thought of working in a factory,
> but he also knows Joanne dislikes the farm. After several
> days of anxious indecision, Tom persuades Joanne to
> stay on the farm.

The difference between this paragraph and the story are obvious. One is a plot summary, the other a fully developed story. One relies only on exposition; the other includes dialogue, thoughts, actions, and description, in addition to exposition. One "tells" us about a man and events; the other allows us to partially experience those events and identify more easily with the central character.

The next student story, "Jennifer," is a more subtly drawn piece of fiction. The conflict and central concern are not obviously stated, and you may, in fact, have to read the story more than once before you comprehend its full meaning.

JENNIFER

Jennifer gratefully sipped her iced tea. The afternoon was hot and dry, and she felt its weight like an unseen hand bearing down on her mind. Placing her glass on the arm of her patio chair, she looked up, and in a sweeping glance took in the view before her. Her brows knit as she realized how brown and ragged the lawn had become. The carefully laid sod covering the gentle sloping lawn that fell from the flagstone patio, even the hedge that marked the boundaries of their property, needed attention. Turning in her chair, she was surprised by the disorder that had begun to curl around the edges of the terraced garden that flanked the right side of the patio. She sat up in her chair a little, took in the landscape deliberately for another second, and made a mental note to hire a gardener for the first of next week. She didn't feel up to gardening now and wasn't sure, anyway, just how to approach these ragged blooms. Jason had never allowed anyone but himself to care for the yard.

Jennifer turned her attention to the gracious graystone house that loomed up in back of her and checked her watch for the third time in less than an hour. "I wonder if she'll be much longer? It's been over half an hour since she went up to Jason's room." Jennifer's musings set her mind on the situation upstairs. She had thought it only proper that Jason's mother be asked to look over his personal things to see if there were any items she might want to keep . . . to treasure. Jason was all she had left, and he and his mother had been so close. She had been Jason's closest business confidante even though she had no controlling interest in the firm. She was looking out for Jason's future. That's what she said.

And his future had been secure, Jennifer thought. This lovely home, one of the town's leading businessmen, family and social life in order. At the peak at thirty-five and then . . . Who could have anticipated a heart attack? Who . . . .

"Dear, I think I'll be leaving now."

Jennifer turned and saw her mother-in-law framed in the stone arch of the patio entrance. As the older woman stepped into the light, it betrayed the number of sleepless nights and long days that her son's death had brought. "She looks so small, so vulnerable now," Jennifer thought as she rose in greeting.

"Mother, are you all right?" She reached out and pulled a second chair over near her own and motioned for her mother-in-law to sit down. She walked over to the serving cart that stood at the patio's edge and poured a glass of tea.

"It must have been hard for you," Jennifer offered as she extended the glass of tea in Mrs. Adams' direction, "going through his things like that."

"Yes. I just couldn't bring myself to come before. And thank you, Jennifer. Thank you for asking me. I remembered so many things up there just now. His ski jacket. How he enjoyed skiing. It wasn't that he didn't get enough exercise, you know. And when I saw his golf jacket—thrown over the chair like he'd just come from the club . . . ."

She paused, her voice out of control for a moment. Jennifer looked across the lawn at the still scene before her. Nothing moved or seemed to breathe for several seconds.

"I took very little, really."

Jennifer nodded as her mother-in-law continued. "The cuff links . . . the ones I gave him on his last birthday. Remember, he had just returned from the Bahamas."

Mrs. Adams checked herself. Her hand drifted to her throat and then nervously played with the collar on her starched shirtwaist dress. She eyed the younger woman carefully.

"Dear, I wasn't thinking. How thoughtless of me to go on about Jason that way."

Jennifer looked down at her hands. Her thin face was composed even though her eyes also spoke of sleepless nights and a small gray pain still not exorcised. She stood up, shaking her head lightly and her brown hair danced for a moment in the still air. She smiled and then reached across to the older woman.

"It's all right."

The two women touched for a moment, Mrs. Adams studied Jennifer's face once again and then took a careful breath. "Dear, I see you've moved into the guest room. I think that's a sensible move. So depressing to stay in the master bedroom with all . . . ."

Jennifer turned away for a moment and the patio was once again shrouded in an awkward silence.

The sound of tennis shoes slapping on the driveway called the women's attention. A young figure, lean and brown and clad in jeans and a striped T-shirt, approached the edge of the patio garden and tossed a neatly rolled paper at the doorstep that lay just beyond the entrance arch.

"Hi, Mrs. Adams."

"Hi, David." Jennifer's face brightened as she followed the agile figure. In a flash he was gone, running back down the drive. Jennifer thought she could almost feel his heart flutter in time to the pump, pump of those soiled sneakers.

"That's Chuck McClure's son, isn't it?"

"Yes, Mother Adams."

"Why, Chuck and Jason went to scool together . . . ." A sob choked the older woman's voice again.

"Mother, don't."

"But Jennifer, if only you and Jason had had children. I know he was anxious to get himself settled. But if only . . . ."

"Don't think about it now."

Mrs. Adams forced a tight smile and stood up with a sigh. "Jennifer, I think you're right. And Aunt Clive and I have been thinking about you. It's been over two months since Jason died. It's all right for two foolish old ladies like us to mope around and live in the past. But you're so young. We have been so pleased with the way you've adjusted. You've been so strong, Jennifer. Well, don't you think it's about time you got out a bit. Perhaps to the club with some old friends. This house is so big and empty."

Jennifer's body visibly stiffened at the suggestion and her voice took on an uncharacteristic briskness as she spoke. "It just isn't time yet." She rose from her chair as she spoke and walked over to the potted geraniums that skirted the edge of the patio. Her shoulders refused to relax as the older woman paused at her side a moment before she turned to go.

Jennifer showered early and dressed in a fresh yellow summer dress. She intended to eat early in the library and spend the rest of the evening attending to correspondence.

As she entered the library, she saw that Molly, her cook and light housekeeper, had her tray ready. Jennifer settled down in a comfortable corner chair and began to eat. The late summer sun played on the dark paneling on the walls, giving the room an added richness. She took no particular note of what she ate but was nonetheless totally absorbed in her meal, so that she failed to notice Molly standing in the doorway.

At last the gray-haired, aging woman knocked timidly on the door casing. "Ma'am, can I get you more tea?"

"No thank you, Molly. The meal is just fine. I'll be in the library the rest of the evening. I must attend to the last of these condolence messages. So many of Mr. Adams' associates sent personal cards. I really must send a personal thank you."

"Oh, Mrs. Your Mr. Adams would be so proud of you. He always liked things proper."

"Yes," Jennifer remarked absently. She hadn't meant to talk over these things with Molly. But what did it matter after all. Suddenly, as if she pulled herself out of a daze, "Molly, that's all for now."

Jennifer stayed in the library and worked at a small desk that sat in the corner of the room. She wrote into the gathering twilight, composing messages in her small, even script.

Midway through the correspondence she paused. She was surprised to read a personal note from Senator Clymins. Why a personal note from a Washington senator should surprise her, she did not know. But she touched the envelope, feeling its smoothness, and was rereading the note for a second time when Molly interrupted her.

"Ma'am, it's after nine. I'll be going now. Do you need me tomorrow?"

"No, Molly, you needn't return until Monday. Goodnight."

As the echo of the closing kitchen door vibrated through the house, Jennifer thought about tomorrow. Tomorrow is Saturday. Time for baseball and picnics and all those family things that echoed across the streets and up her front lawn, assaulting her own ordered world with noisy laughter.

She pushed the cards back. "It's time to quit," she spoke aloud and was startled by the sound of her own voice in the stillness. "It's time," she whispered, but she didn't finish the thought this time, if indeed she knew what the completed thought should be. Instead she put out the lights in the library and then in the dining room as she walked the short distance to the circular stair. She knew that Molly would have locked the doors before leaving, so she proceeded upstairs.

Once on the second floor, Jennifer paused long enough to shut the door to the master bedroom and continued to the end of the hall where the guest room was. As she opened the door, the sight of her personal things greeted her warmly. "It's good to be home," she mused and then laughed quietly at her reaction. Moving to the small dressing table that stood against the far wall, she sat in front of the mirror for a moment and looked at the image in the mirror. She could still make out the outlines of her face and shoulders by the light of the street lamps that stood in front of the house. With a careless gesture she pushed her hair aside and then began unbuttoning her dress.

Laying the dress across the corner of the table, she stood and then let her nylon half-slip slide down her legs and fall in a puddle around her feet. "Is it time?" she questioned. "I don't know. I just don't know."

With the grace of a dancer, Jennifer crossed the room, dressed now in a simple, light nightgown. She adjusted the window so that the timid breeze that was beginning to stir outside could invade her room.

"How long have I looked at this view, the front yard and out across the town. How many times have I seen the lights blink out, one after another, until all the world was asleep but me. It's been nearly a year," she thought. Jennifer had come here when the first snow had lain heavy on the trees. And she had been able to find some delight in the coming of spring. It had been so beautiful from these windows, and Jennifer found a private pleasure in the budding trees and the first robin framed by her window like a greeting card portrait. Jason had called this her little retreat and had said no more. He went on with life and calmly waited for her return. Day after day he waited confidently until the promise of summer's ripeness taunted her. As summer began to break Jason seemed taunted, too, and then . . .

She turned from the window, remembering the past two months, remembering Jason's funeral, remembering how she had grieved and had been surprised by her grief.

But now . . . . Now she realized, as she took in the quiet night before her, she had only to watch the coming of autumn from this window and the cycle would be complete.

The telephone startled Jennifer back into her room. She paused, half wishing to forget it. It was still early enough to be a belated condolence call or her mother-in-law or perhaps someone from the club again, insisting that she join them for a late evening drink.

Jennifer stood there, holding onto the delicate curtain as the ringing died away. She turned carefully and quietly back to the window and pulled the curtain aside for one last look at the deepening shadows that stretched across the front lawn. The lights of the town began blinking out one by one. A breeze gently stirred the curtain in her hand. She looked across the lawn to the sycamore and oak trees that lined the drive, and wondered at the two small, still pliable leaves that floated on the night breeze to the ground.

There is very little exposition in this story. The conflict and central concern are not readily apparent. Several facts become clear as the story progresses. Jennifer's husband Jason had died two months earlier; his mother is more demonstrative about her bereavement than his wife is; and Jennifer has been sleeping in the guest room for several months prior to Jason's death. Some of the important information is not directly stated, but instead is communicated more subtly in the selection of language and the things Jennifer leaves unsaid.

Notice, for example, that the setting is not extraneous to the meaning of the story. The setting helps to suggest some things about Jennifer's past life and present state of mind. I used the opening paragraph of this story in Chapter 4 to illustrate how a writer can use setting to reinforce characterization. Of course, the full significance of this paragraph does not become apparent until later in the story. The hot, dry weather, the unkempt yard, and the ragged blooms echo the arid, barrenness of Jennifer's life with Jason. The boundaries of the yard and of Jennifer's life need attention. Now that Jason is dead, Jennifer must take charge of her life, as well as the yard.

In Chapter 5 I discussed indirect characterization. We indirectly learn a great deal about Jennifer and Jason in this story. We are not told, for instance, that Jason always cared for the lawn. Rather we are told that he had "never allowed anyone but himself to care for the yard." The implication is that Jason was the one who made the rules. He was also close to his mother and Jennifer's resentment of that fact is evident in her reflection about her mother-in-law. "She was looking out for Jason's future. That's what she said." The last sentence adds an ironic twist to what otherwise might be simply a statement of fact. The mother's attachment to her son is also emphasized in her continued anguish two months after his death. In contrast, Jennifer, though she grieved, was not overly distressed by Jason's death and now, except for a lingering "small gray pain" she is calm and composed. She apparently had never fully accepted the "proper," sexless, childless marriage. It is clear from her response to the newsboy that she would have enjoyed having children. During the time that the story takes place, Jennifer is simply putting the finishing touches on her past life. She does the "proper" thing with her mother-in-law; she carefully composes responses to condolence messages; and she even seems to savor the privacy of her "own ordered world." She is finishing out the "cycle" of her break with Jason. At the same time she is hesitant and perhaps a little afraid of beginning a new life.

Very little of what we learn in this story is told to us directly in exposition. Instead the writer relies heavily on the other narrative methods. The descriptive details, the dialogue, and the carefully chosen language guide our responses, but we are left to draw the intended conclusions about Jennifer's character and her marriage to Jason.

The ending of this story may confuse you. Both this and the previous story are a bit weak in the resolutions. "Summer Holocaust" ends too quickly, too easily, and "Jennifer" perhaps ends a bit too obscurely. Though she has admitted that it is time to stop her old life, Jennifer is indecisive and reluctant to begin a new life. She clearly refuses to socialize with old friends at the club— Jason's friends, no doubt. But we are not sure what she will do. The description of the falling leaves in the final sentence is somewhat ambiguous. They may signal the end of her previous life style, but they may also signal her inability to leave her sheltered existence.

All three of the stories we have discussed in this chapter are relatively sophisticated in their use of fictional techniques. Though the content of all fiction is composed from the same basic elements, the way writers use these elements can vary considerably from story to story. It is this difference in presentation that distinguishes simple fiction from sophisticated or complex fiction. As Stephen Minot explains, complex fictional works "do" more "in the sense that they suggest more, imply a greater range of suggestions, develop more subtle shadings of meaning."[1] In simple fiction, plots are

[1] *Three Genres: The Writing of Poetry, Fiction, and Drama,* 2d ed. (Englewood Cliffs, N.J.: Prentice-Hall, 1971), p. 130.

conventional and direct; characters do a lot but tend to be superficial and one dimensional; settings are not used to reinforce the story's central concern; and the thematic focus can often be reduced to a "moral" rather than offering suggestions about the nature of life or existence.

I have said that this chapter is not intended to focus exclusively on fiction writing, but is meant rather to point the way from personal writing to fiction. It undoubtedly has not answered all your questions, but perhaps it has made you more aware of the essential differences between autobiographical papers and fiction. You may also better understand the importance of controlling the basic fictional elements when you metamorphose a personal experience into a story. As a fiction writer you will probably become more acutely aware of the technical achievements in professional stories. How does a writer, for instance, move smoothly and unobtrusively from exposition to dramatization? How does a writer handle the third-person point of view so that it reads easily but not like a scientific report or a news article? These are questions you may begin asking as you try writing your own fiction. For answers you will probably turn to examples of professional writing with a new awareness and appreciation. Certainly the reader who has tried to write fiction is often more perceptive about the literary achievement of others.

The importance of revision in all your writing should be obvious by now. Like most of the writing done within the confines of a class, your fiction papers might be viewed as working papers. As a novice fiction writer, you are not expected to produce a publishable story in the last few weeks of a term. What you will want to do, however, is to practice fictional techniques, by first producing working papers for class discussion and later by offering revised working papers. The initial discussions of papers can focus on which fictional tools are being used effectively and which need to be improved. In the course of these discussions you can sharpen your understanding of the nature and structure of sophisticated fiction. If you are seriously interested in writing—either fiction or other modes—you will continue to write, to ask for critical response, and to revise in light of those responses. Eventually, you will become a reliable and perceptive critic of your own writing.

A 5
B 6
C 7
D 8
E 9
F 0
G 1
H 2
I 3
J 4